SKILL SHARPENERS

Science

1

Contents

How to Use This Book 6

Physical Science

Sound 8

Concept: Forces can make objects vibrate, and vibrations make sound.

Skills: Match graphic images to science concepts; Match graphic images to words; Read science words; Visual discrimination; Apply science vocabulary in context sentences; Conduct experiments and record observations

Light 16

Concept: There are different sources of light.

Skills: Match graphic images to words; Match graphic images to science concepts; Read science words; Visual discrimination; Apply science vocabulary in context sentences; Apply science concepts to real-world situations

Shadows 24

Concept: Shadows are produced when a light source is blocked.

Skills: Match graphic images to words; Visual discrimination; Read science words; Apply science vocabulary in context sentences; Make art projects to represent science concepts; Make scientific observations and record information

Technology 32

Concept: We use technology to communicate.

Skills: Match graphic images to words; Read science words; Visual discrimination; Apply science vocabulary in context sentences; Apply science concepts to real-world situations

Life Science

Leaves 40

Concept: Leaves help trees survive and grow.

Skills: Label graphic images to demonstrate understanding of science concepts; Visual discrimination; Read science words; Apply science vocabulary in context sentences; Make art projects to represent science concepts

Animals and Eggs **48**

Concept: Some animals lay eggs.

Skills: Match graphic images to words; Label graphic images to demonstrate understanding of science concepts; Read science words; Visual discrimination; Apply science vocabulary in context sentences; Make art projects to represent science concepts

Mothers and Babies **56**

Concept: Some animal babies look like their mothers, but others do not.

Skills: Match graphic images to words; Match graphic images to demonstrate understanding of science concepts; Read science words; Visual discrimination; Apply science vocabulary in context sentences; Make art projects to represent science concepts; Apply science concepts to real-world situations

Birds **64**

Concept: Animals have body parts that help them survive.

Skills: Match graphic images to words; Interpret information from charts or graphs; Read science words; Visual discrimination; Apply science vocabulary in context sentences; Do research to write and illustrate informational text

Insects **72**

Concept: Insects are the same in many ways, but they are also different.

Skills: Match graphic images to words; Label graphic images to demonstrate understanding of science concepts; Read science words; Visual discrimination; Apply science vocabulary in context sentences; Make real-world observations and write about them

Space and Earth Science

Night Sky **80**

Concept: The moon and stars are objects in the sky.

Skills: Match graphic images to words; Match graphic images to science concepts; Read science words; Visual discrimination; Apply science vocabulary in context sentences; Make art projects to represent science concepts

Our Sun **88**

Concept: People, plants, and animals need the sun's heat and light.

Skills: Match graphic images to words; Read science words; Visual discrimination; Apply science vocabulary in context sentences; Make real-world observations and write about them

Seasons 96

Concept: Weather changes from season to season.

Skills: Match graphic images to words; Match graphic images to science concepts; Read science words; Visual discrimination; Apply science vocabulary in context sentences; Make art projects to represent science concepts

Environment and Ecology Science

Uses of Wood 104

Concept: Trees provide material for many products.

Skills: Match graphic images to words; Match graphic images to science concepts; Read science words; Visual discrimination; Apply science vocabulary in context sentences; Make real-world observations and write about them; Make art projects to represent science concepts

Earth Materials 112

Concept: Earth has natural resources.

Skills: Match graphic images to words; Match graphic images to science concepts; Read science words; Visual discrimination; Apply science vocabulary in context sentences; Draw pictures to represent science concepts

Recycling 120

Concept: Recycling can reduce our impact on the environment.

Skills: Match graphic images to words; Match graphic images to science concepts; Read science words; Visual discrimination; Apply science vocabulary in context sentences; Make art projects to represent science concepts

Engineering and Design

Tools 128

Concept: The shape and design of a tool are related to its function.

Skills: Match graphic images to words; Match graphic images to science concepts; Read science words; Visual discrimination; Apply science vocabulary in context sentences; Make projects to represent science concepts

Answer Key 136

How to Use This Book

Learning About Science

Science is all around us, and children are naturally curious about their world. They investigate, problem solve, experiment, and imagine new ways to do things—they are, by nature, scientists! Studies show that children learn best through hands-on experiences. As your child asks questions about the world, you may look to science to answer some of those questions. This book will help you connect your child's real-world experiences to science concepts and vocabulary.

The lessons in this book provide information and activities about physical, life, and earth sciences in addition to science and engineering careers.

Reading Selections

Read the selection to your child. Point to vocabulary words and have your child say each word aloud. Discuss how the illustrations or photos help your child better understand the science concept. Then, if your child is able, have him or her read the selection to you.

Visual Literacy

Illustrations and photos help your child relate science concepts to the real world. Use the visual literacy activities to reinforce the science concepts that were presented in the reading selection. Provide your child with support by reading the directions aloud and answering any questions he or she may have about the activity.

Vocabulary

The vocabulary activities range from word puzzles to writing vocabulary words to complete sentences. Provide your child with support by reading the directions aloud and answering any questions he or she may have about the activity.

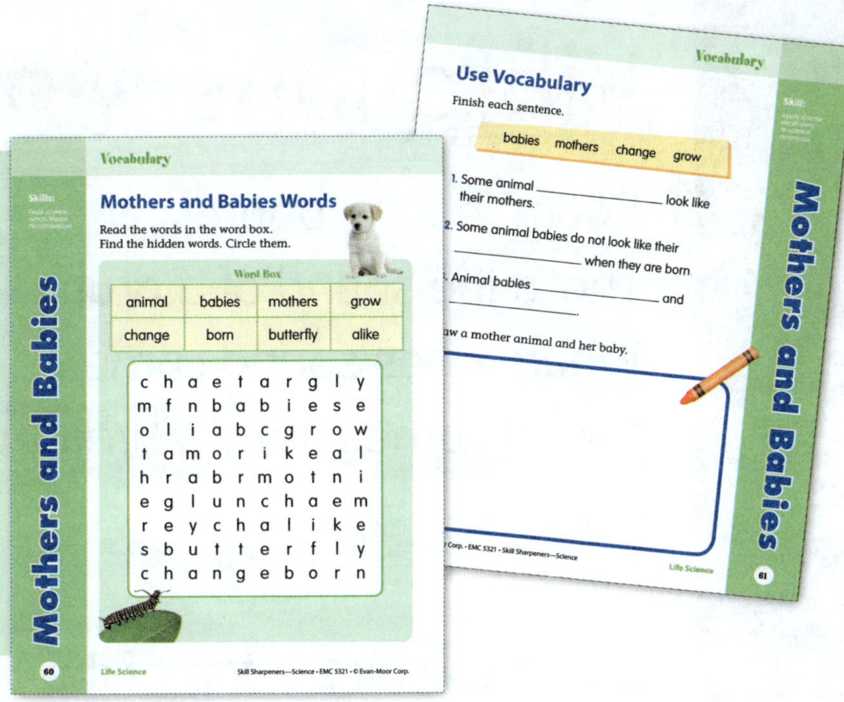
Vocabulary

Mothers and Babies Words

Read the words in the word box.
Find the hidden words. Circle them.

Word Box

animal	babies	mothers	grow
change	born	butterfly	alike

c h a e t a r g l y
m f n b a b i e s e
o l i a b c g r o w
t a m o r i k e a l
h r a b r m o t n i
e g l u n c h a e m
r e y c h a l i k e
s b u t t e r f l y
c h a n g e b o r n

Mothers and Babies

60 Life Science Skill Sharpeners—Science • EMC 5321 • © Evan-Moor Corp.

Vocabulary

Use Vocabulary

Finish each sentence.

babies mothers change grow

1. Some animal ______ look like their mothers.
2. Some animal babies do not look like their ______ when they are born.
Animal babies ______ and ______.
aw a mother animal and her baby.

Mothers and Babies

Life Science 61

Hands-on Activities

The hands-on activities provide your child with opportunities to connect science concepts to the real world. The activities focus on developing process skills such as observing, collecting, and organizing information. In addition, you and your child will create projects that bring science concepts to life. These activities are designed for parents and children to complete together.

Hands-on Activity

At the Pet Store

Visit a local pet store to see tadpoles and frogs.

Draw pictures of what you saw.

Tadpole Frog

Mothers and Babies

Life Science 63

Hands-on Activity

Mother and Baby

Draw a picture of a mother and her baby.

What You Need
- paper
- crayons or colored pencils

What You Do
1. Choose an animal mother and baby to draw.
2. Draw a picture of the animal mother and her baby.
3. Write a sentence that tells how they are alike or different.
4. Show your picture to someone and explain how they are alike or different.

Mothers and Babies

62 Life Science Skill Sharpeners—Science • EMC 5321 • © Evan-Moor Corp.

Concept:

Forces can make objects vibrate, and vibrations make sound.

Vibrations Make Sound

Boom, boom, boom!
That's the sound of a drum.
Where does sound come from?
Sound comes from **vibrations**.

When you hit the top of the drum, it will vibrate, or move over and over very fast.

As the drum vibrates, it makes **sound waves** that move through the air.

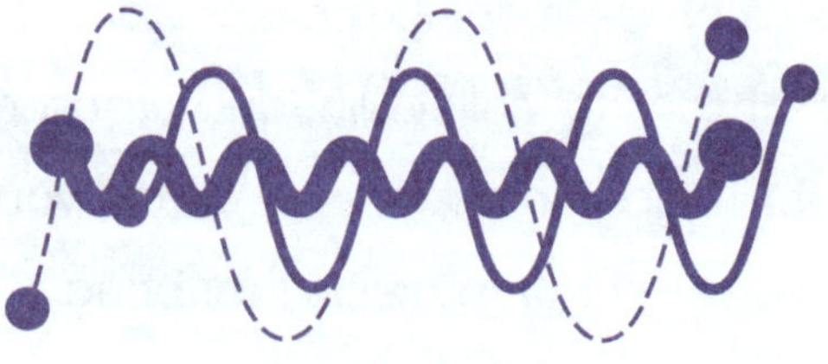

Some sound waves are **musical**.

Sound

We **pluck**
some instruments
to make sound.

We **blow**
some instruments
to make sound.

We **hit**
some instruments
to make sound.

We **shake**
some instruments
to make sound.

Skill:

Match graphic images to science concepts

Sound

Sound Match

Draw a line to match.

sound waves

musical

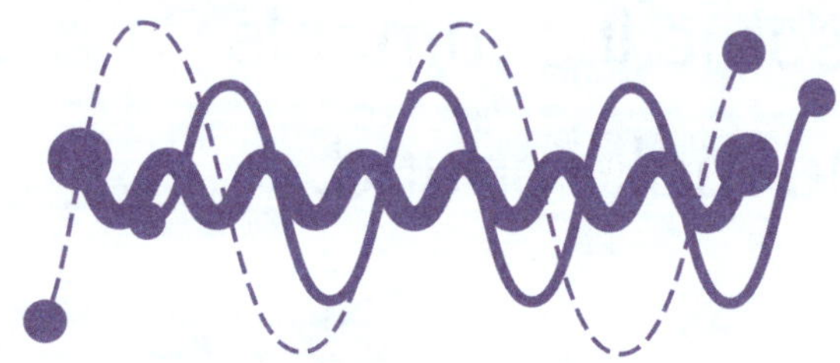

vibrations

Finish the sentence.

Sound comes from ______________________.

Making Sound

Skill:

Match graphic images to words

Draw a line to match.

hit

pluck

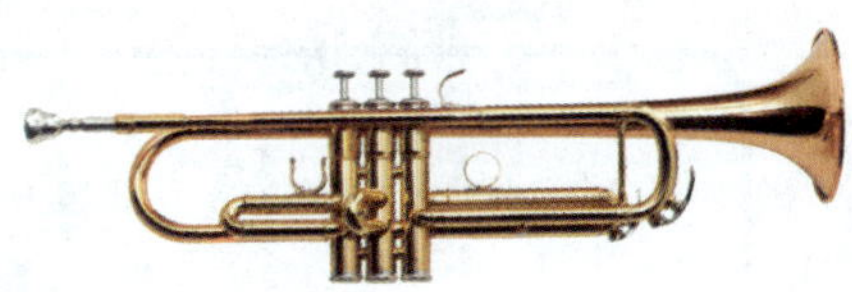

blow

shake

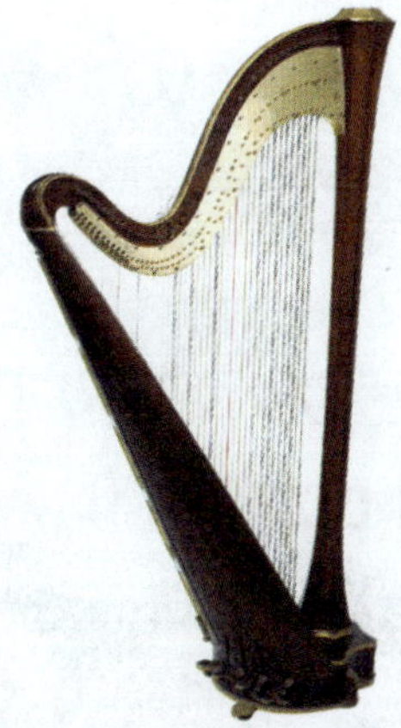

Skills:

Read science words; Visual discrimination

Sound Words

Read the words in the word box.
Find the hidden words. Circle them.

Word Box

pluck	hit	vibrations	musical
shake	blow	sound	move

v i b r a t i o n s
b l a m v r c h p w
x m u s i c a l l v
h v d c t s o u u a
i a s h a k e a c e
t m o o l c e v k s
u o s e b n n l p o
d v v i b l o w e u
m e c r k e v l t n
b a i o n w i v a d

Use Vocabulary

Finish each sentence.

vibrates move sound

1. When you hit a drum, it ____________________.
2. The vibrations make ____________________.
3. Sound waves ____________________ through the air.

Draw an instrument you **blow** to make sound.

Skill:

Apply science vocabulary in context sentences

Sound

Skill:
Conduct experiments and record observations

Listen to Vibrations

Use objects from your house to make sounds.

What You Need

Set 1

- a wooden spoon
- a fork
- your hand

Set 2

- a glass vase or jar
- a plastic bowl or container
- a metal pan

What You Do

1. Use each item in Set 1 to tap lightly on an item from Set 2. Notice how the vibrations you create make a different sound for each object.

2. Draw an X in the chart after you try each item.

wooden spoon 	◯ glass	◯ metal	◯ plastic
fork 	◯ glass	◯ metal	◯ plastic
hand 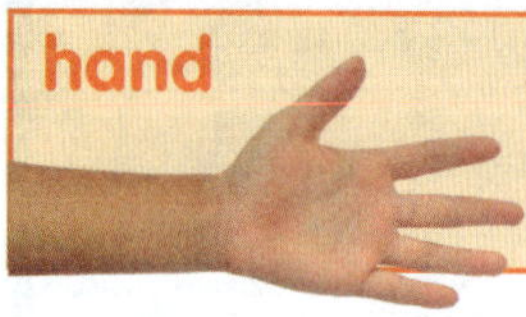	◯ glass	◯ metal	◯ plastic

Making Sounds

Skill: Conduct experiments and record observations

Put objects into a cup and shake it up!

What You Need

- an empty paper cup with a lid
- objects that fit inside the cup: uncooked rice or beans, coins, board game pieces, cotton balls, cord or yarn, etc.

What You Do

1. Put one group of objects inside the cup. Place the lid on the cup and shake it up. Listen to the sound.
2. Empty the cup and put a different group of objects in it. Repeat until you have experimented with all the objects.
3. Draw which objects made loud or quiet sounds.

These made a **loud** sound.	These made a **quiet** sound.

Concept:

There are different sources of light.

Light

Light is all around us.

Some light comes from nature.

sun

moon

stars

Some light comes from things that people make.

candles

flashlight

lamp

Light helps us see.
If we did not have light,
the world would be dark.

Light helps us live.
People, animals, and
plants need light.

Light

Skill:

Match graphic images to words

Light Match

Draw a line to match.

candle

sun

lamp

moon

Finish the sentence.

Light helps us ______________________.

Who Makes It?

Skill:

Match graphic images to science concepts

Look at the picture. Check the correct box.

nature    people 

nature ◯ people ◯

nature ◯ people ◯

nature ◯ people ◯

nature ◯ people ◯

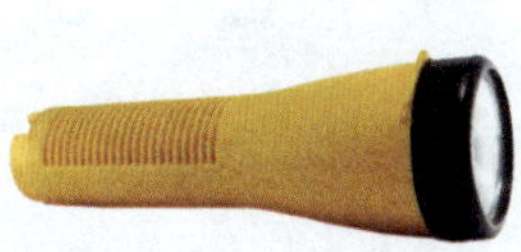

nature ◯ people ◯

nature ◯ people ◯

Light

Skills:

Read science words; Visual discrimination

Light Words

Read the words in the word box.
Find the hidden words. Circle them.

Word Box

nature	light	live	dark
moon	stars	lamp	candle

l i n d m o o n k a
f g c e s d l h n l
e l a m p o i s g i
c h n a t u r e t v
a t r k i d m f s e
n a l i g h t e l k
d g s f v i n t d a
l n d a r k d v e o
e l a o b s t a r s

Use Vocabulary

Skill:
Apply science vocabulary in context sentences

Finish each sentence.

light　　nature　　live

1. Some light comes from ______________.
2. If we did not have ______________, the world would be dark.
3. Light helps us ______________.

Draw light that comes from nature.

Skill:

Apply science concepts to real-world situations

Lights Inside

Your house has light from things that people made. Draw four lights that people made and write the names.

Light

Lights Outside

You can see light from nature outside. Draw three sources of light from nature and write the names.

Skill:

Apply science concepts to real-world situations

Concept:

Shadows are produced when a light source is blocked.

Light and Shadows

Light moves in a line.

Light can move through some things.

Light moves through glass.

Light cannot move

through other things.

Light does not move

through a ball.

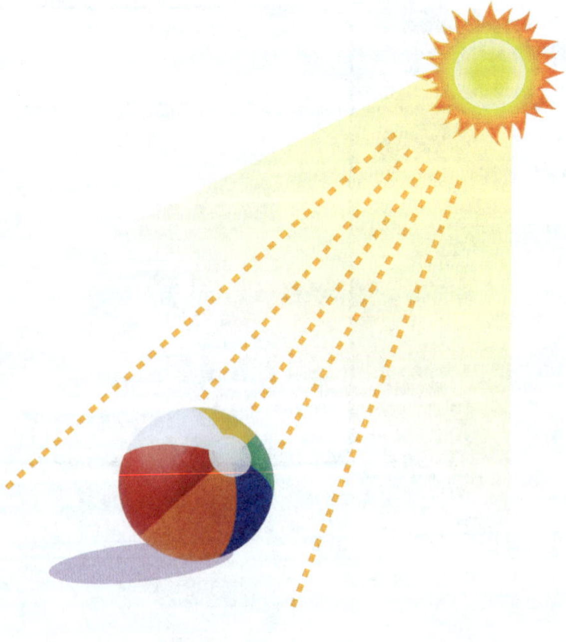

When light cannot move through something, you may see a shadow.

A shadow is a dark spot.

Shadows

Skill:

Match graphic images to words

Shadow Match

Draw a line to match.

shadow

glass

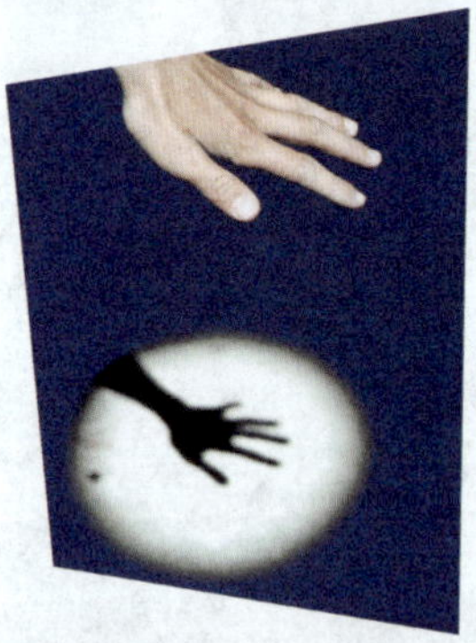

light

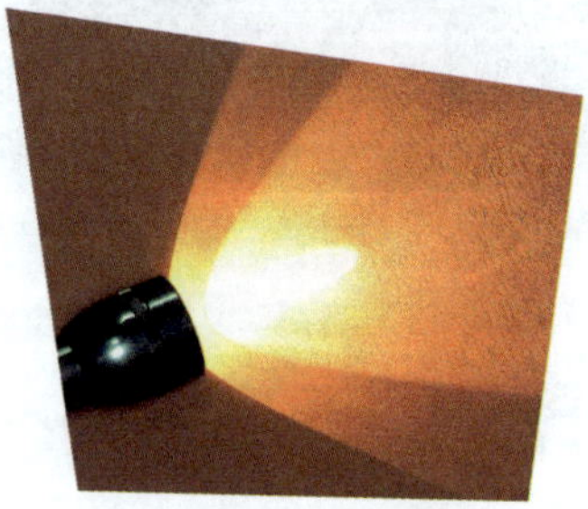

Finish the sentence.

When light cannot move through something,

it makes a ______________________.

Shadows

What Made the Shadow?

Skill:
Visual discrimination

Draw a line to match.

Skills:

Read science words; Visual discrimination

Shadow and Light Words

Read the words in the word box.
Find the hidden words. Circle them.

Word Box

shadow	light	glass	dark
through	shine	line	move

d r k o u m g l s i
a s h a d o w n e d
l g t n u v r t c a
i s h i n e k h v r
g a r t h o n r u k
h e g l a s s o r t
t a c h r o k u d l
s l i n e v d g o e
t o w d h i t h e k

Use Vocabulary

Skill:
Apply science vocabulary in context sentences

Finish each sentence.

light	line	shadow

1. Light moves in a ________________________.
2. ________________________ cannot move through some things.
3. A ________________________ is a dark spot.

Draw an object or person that has a shadow.

Skill:

Make art projects to represent science concepts

Shadows

Shadow Art

Create a picture that has a shadow.

What You Need

- black, white, and light-colored construction paper
- crayons
- scissors
- glue

What You Do

1. Draw a picture of an object or person on the white paper.
2. Put the black piece of paper behind the white paper. Hold both pieces of paper together as you cut out your drawing.

3. Draw a sun on the light-colored construction paper. Glue your drawing onto the paper. Glue the shadow onto the paper.
4. Write a sentence that tells what the picture shows.

Shadow Walk

Skill:
Make scientific observations and record information

Go outside and find shadows.

What You Need

- a camera

What You Do

1. On a sunny day, get a camera and go for a walk.
2. Look for shadows outside. When you see a shadow, take a picture of it.
3. After you get home, look through your pictures and answer the questions below.

Draw and write to answer the questions.

1. What shadow did you like best? Draw it.

2. What did it show? ______________________________

3. Why was there a shadow? __________________________

____

Shadows

Concept:

We use technology to communicate.

Technology

We use technology to read, play games, look and listen, and talk to each other.

These things are technology:

computer

cellphone

tablet

television

People use technology to learn.

People use technology to have fun.

Skill:
Match graphic images to words

Tech Match

Draw a line to match.

cellphone

computer

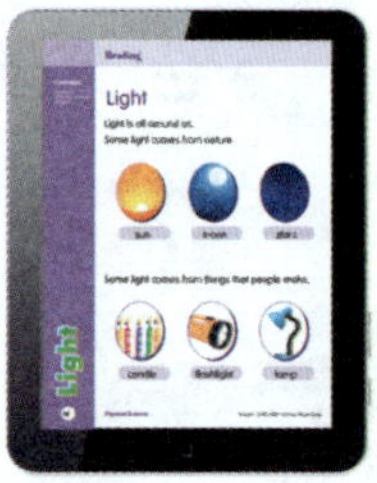

television

tablet

Finish the sentence.

These things are ______________________.

Technology

Technology

Draw a line to match.

talk

play

learn

look and listen

Skill:

Match graphic images to words

Technology

Skills:

Read science words; Visual discrimination

Technology Words

Read the words in the word box.
Find the hidden words. Circle them.

Word Box

tablet	computer	television	cellphone
fun	play	learn	technology

c m p o t f u n r l
t e l e v i s i o n
a l e a r n t v e m
b f u l y p h o e p
l c o m p u t e r l
e l l g y c a m r a
t f n o u t e v n y
c e l l p h o n e r
t e c h n o l o g y

Technology

Use Vocabulary

Skill:
Apply science vocabulary in context sentences

Finish each sentence.

learn   technology   talk

1. People use ____________________ to read.
2. People use technology to ____________________.
3. People use technology to ____________________ to each other.

Draw a picture of your favorite technology.

Skill:

Apply science concepts to real-world situations

Technology at Home

Does your family use technology at home? Draw 4 kinds of technology you use at home and write the names.

Technology

Technology at School

Does your school use technology? Draw 4 kinds of technology you use at school and write the names.

Skill:

Apply science concepts to real-world situations

Technology

Concept:

Leaves help trees survive and grow.

All Kinds of Leaves

Leaves help trees grow and live.
Trees grow leaves of many shapes and sizes.

Leaves

Leaves look different.

But they have the same parts.

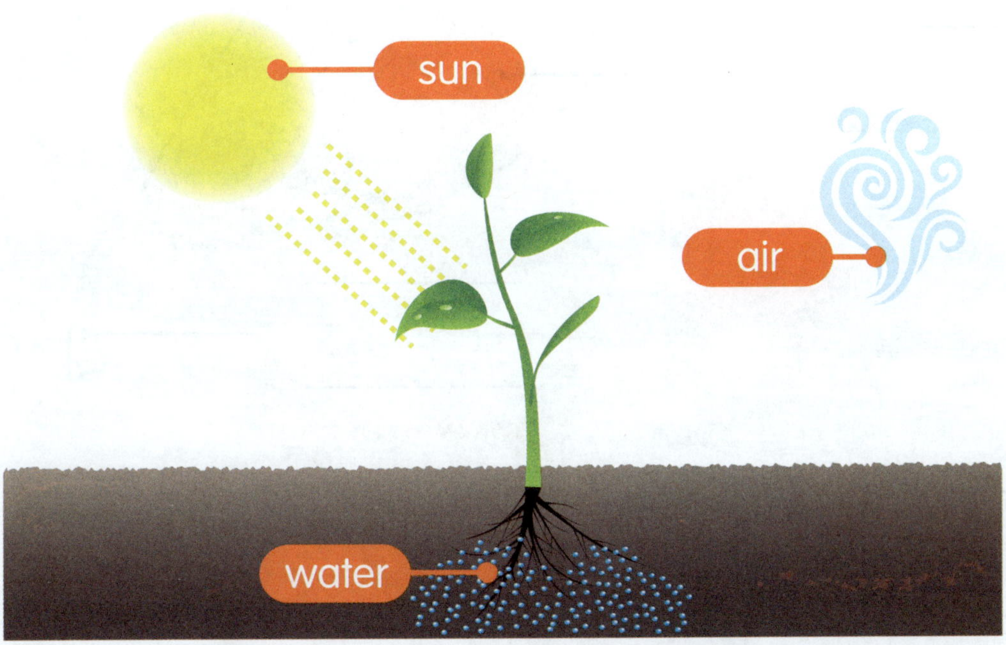

Leaves make food for the tree. They make food from the sun, air, and water.

Leaves

Skill:

Label graphic images to demonstrate understanding of science concepts

Leaf Parts

Trace each word to label the leaf parts.

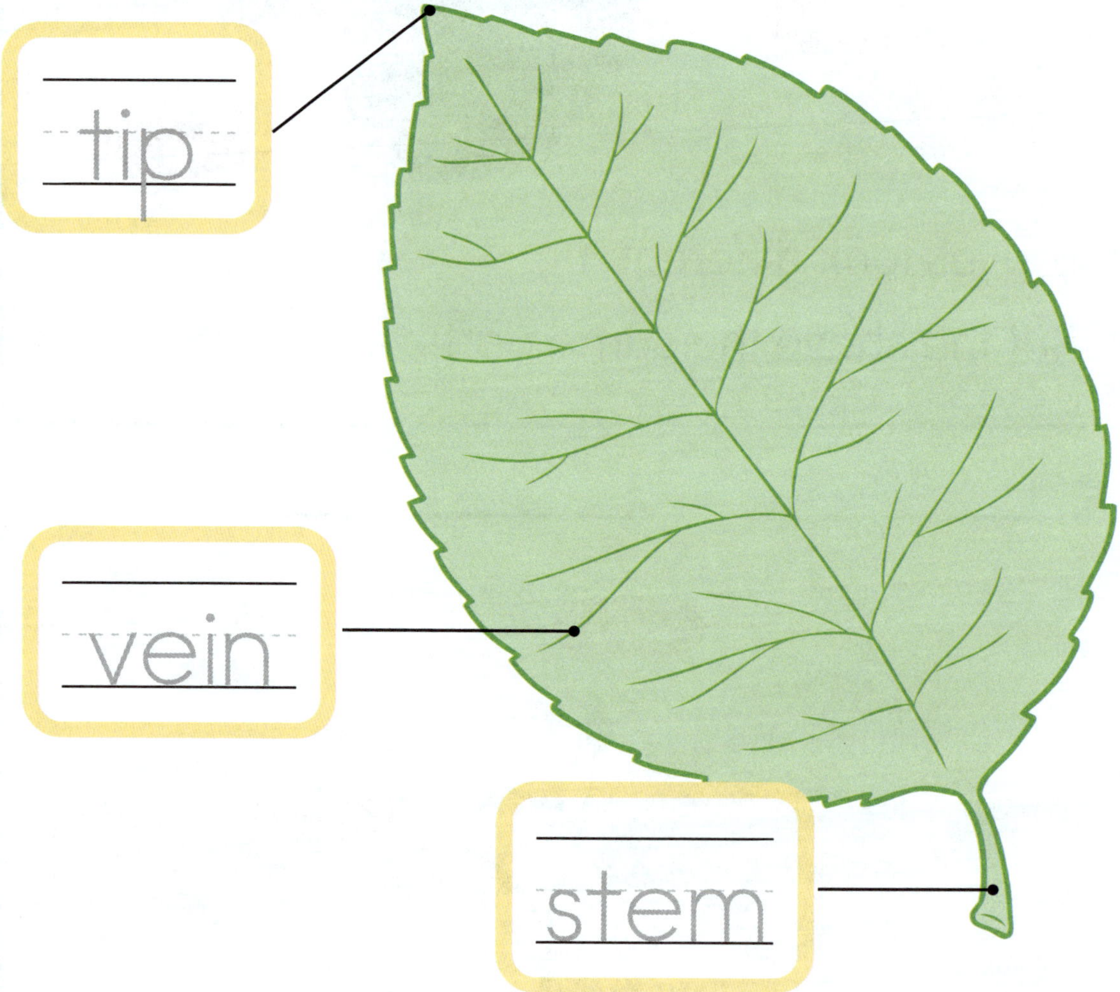

Finish the sentence.

Leaves help trees grow and ______________________.

Leaves

Leaves Have Shapes

Skill: Visual discrimination

Draw a line to match.

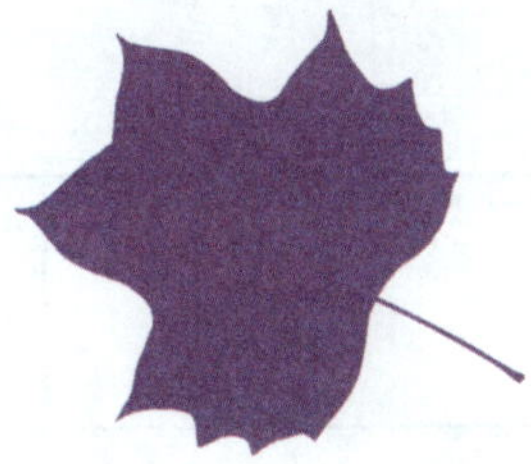

Skills:

Read science words; Visual discrimination

Leaf Words

Unscramble the words about leaves.
Write the words in the boxes.

Word Box

tip	leaf	tree	sizes
leaves	live	shapes	grow

- sevale
- fael
- eret
- izsse
- ipt
- viel
- phesas
- wogr

Use Vocabulary

Finish each sentence.

trees	live	food

1. Leaves help trees grow and ______________________.

2. ______________________ grow leaves of many shapes and sizes.

3. Leaves make ______________________ for the tree.

Draw your favorite leaf.

Skill:

Apply science vocabulary in context sentences

Leaves

Skill:

Make art projects to represent science concepts

Leaf Rubbings

Use real leaves to make a picture!

What You Need

- paper bag
- leaves of different shapes and sizes
- crayons with wrappers removed
- paper

What You Do

1. Take the paper bag outdoors and collect leaves of different shapes, sizes, and colors.
2. On a hard, flat surface, place a leaf bottom side up on a piece of paper.
3. Put another sheet of paper on top of the leaf.
4. Rub the side of a crayon gently on the area over the leaf. Try to keep the leaf in place with one hand while you color with the other hand.
5. Do the same thing using other crayon colors and leaves.
6. Play with making patterns or your own "tree" of leaves.

Concept:

Some animals lay eggs.

Animals and Eggs

Babies in Eggs

Some animals lay eggs. Their babies grow inside until they are ready to hatch.

bird

turtle

spider

snake

Animals with feathers, scales, or slippery skin lay eggs in many places.

Parents take care of their babies.

They feed them and keep them safe.

Skill:

Match graphic images to words

Animals and Eggs

Egg Match

Draw a line to match.

turtle

spider

bird

snake

Finish the sentence.

Some animals hatch from ______________________.

A Life Cycle

Number the pictures to match.

1. The egg is laid.

2. The egg hatches.

3. The baby is fed.

4. The baby is kept safe.

Skill:

Label graphic images to demonstrate understanding of science concepts

Animals and Eggs

Skills:

Read science words; Visual discrimination

Egg Words

Unscramble the words about eggs.
Write the words in the boxes.

Word Box

eggs	hatch	animals	babies
parents	feed	safe	lay

Use Vocabulary

Skill:
Apply science vocabulary in context sentences

Animals and Eggs

Finish each sentence.

parents eggs hatch

1. Some animals lay ______________.

2. Babies grow in the eggs until they ______________.

3. ______________ take care of their babies.

Draw an animal and its eggs.

Skill:

Make art projects to represent science concepts

Animals and Eggs

What's Hatching Book

Make a book about animals that hatch from eggs!

What You Need

- scissors
- stapler
- crayons, colored pencils, or markers
- 3 sheets of white paper
- 1 sheet of construction paper

What You Do

1. Think about the animals that lay eggs.
2. Look at the pictures of the animals on pages 48–51 of this book.
3. Fold the sheets of white paper and construction paper in half. Staple the folded edge to make a book.
4. Cut out, from a magazine, a photo of an animal that lays eggs. Glue it to the cover of your book. Write a title for your book.
5. On each page of the book, draw a picture of an animal next to its baby hatching from an egg.
6. Write a sentence below each picture you draw.
7. Read your book to someone.

Concept:

Some animal babies look like their mothers, but others do not.

Mothers and Babies

Mothers and Babies

Some animal babies look
a lot like their mothers.

They have the same body parts.
They are the same color.
They are the same shape.

Some babies do not look like
their mothers when they are born.
They look different.

But they will grow and change.

One day, they will look like their mothers, too.

tadpole

froglet

frog

Skill:

Match graphic images to words

Mothers and Babies

Baby Match

Draw a line to match.

puppy

tadpole

caterpillar

kitten

Finish the sentence.

Some animal babies look like their ____________________.

Animals Grow and Change

Skill:

Match graphic images to demonstrate understanding of science concepts

Draw a line to match.

Skills:

Read science words; Visual discrimination

Mothers and Babies

Mothers and Babies Words

Read the words in the word box.
Find the hidden words. Circle them.

Word Box

animal	babies	mothers	grow
change	born	butterfly	alike

c	h	a	e	t	a	r	g	l	y
m	f	n	b	a	b	i	e	s	e
o	l	i	a	b	c	g	r	o	w
t	a	m	o	r	i	k	e	a	l
h	r	a	b	r	m	o	t	n	i
e	g	l	u	n	c	h	a	e	m
r	e	y	c	h	a	l	i	k	e
s	b	u	t	t	e	r	f	l	y
c	h	a	n	g	e	b	o	r	n

Use Vocabulary

Skill:

Apply science vocabulary in context sentences

Finish each sentence.

babies mothers change grow

1. Some animal ____________________ look like their mothers.

2. Some animal babies do not look like their ____________________ when they are born.

3. Animal babies ____________________ and ____________________.

Draw a mother animal and her baby.

Mothers and Babies

Skill:

Make art projects to represent science concepts

Mother and Baby

Draw a picture of a mother and her baby.

What You Need

- paper
- crayons or colored pencils

What You Do

1. Choose an animal mother and baby to draw.
2. Draw a picture of the animal mother and her baby.
3. Write a sentence that tells how they are alike or different.
4. Show your picture to someone and explain how they are alike or different.

At the Pet Store

Visit a local pet store to see tadpoles and frogs.

Draw pictures of what you saw.

Tadpole	Frog

Write about what you saw.

____

____

____

Skill:

Apply science concepts to real-world situations

Mothers and Babies

Concept:

Animals have body parts that help them survive.

Birds of a Feather

Birds come in all colors, shapes, and sizes.
They have body parts that help them live.

Birds have feathers.

Feathers keep a bird warm.
Feathers also keep a bird dry.

Birds

Some birds have webbed feet.

Webbed feet help birds swim.

Birds have beaks.

The shape of a bird's beak helps it eat.
Different birds have different beaks.

Birds are different from one another, but they all have body parts that help them live.

Skill:

Match graphic images to words

Parts of Birds

Draw a line to match.

feathers

webbed feet

long beak

Finish the sentence.

Birds have body parts that help them ______________.

Birds

Different Types of Beaks

Skill: Interpret information from charts or graphs

Read the chart.

Type of Beak	What It Looks Like	What It's Used For
Spear beak		stabbing fish
Scoop beak		scooping fish out of water
Cracker beak		cracking seeds open

1. Which beak is used for scooping fish out of water?

____

2. Which beak is used for cracking seeds?

____

Skills:

Read science words; Visual discrimination

Bird Words

Read the words in the word box.
Find the hidden words. Circle them.

Word Box

birds	feathers	webbed	beaks
feet	swim	body	parts

w	e	b	e	a	k	s	w	e	n
e	f	c	h	d	a	r	p	t	s
h	e	m	w	e	b	b	e	d	w
n	a	f	e	t	r	p	o	b	i
d	t	b	o	d	y	a	k	f	m
b	h	o	y	b	b	r	a	e	t
b	e	s	i	f	a	t	r	e	i
e	r	w	m	e	h	s	b	t	r
p	s	e	b	i	r	d	s	o	d

Use Vocabulary

Skill: Apply science vocabulary in context sentences

Finish each sentence.

webbed feet   feathers   shape

1. Birds have ____________________ to keep them warm and dry.
2. Some birds have ____________________.
3. The ____________________ of a bird's beak helps it eat.

Draw a bird using its beak to eat.

Skill:

Do research to write and illustrate informational text

Bird Facts

Learn more about your favorite bird.

What You Need

- paper
- crayons or colored pencils
- a book about birds, or a computer with an Internet connection

What You Do

1. Go to the library or use the Internet to learn more about birds.
2. Choose your favorite bird.
3. Find out:

◯ what it looks like
◯ where it lives
◯ what it eats
◯ how its body parts help it live

4. Draw and write about it on the next page.

____

bird's name

This bird's beak helps it ________________________.

This bird's wings help it ________________________.

This bird's feet help it ________________________.

Concept:

Insects are the same in many ways, but they are also different.

Insects

Insects are everywhere.

There are many different kinds of insects.

All insects have 3 body parts and 6 legs.

That is what makes them the same.

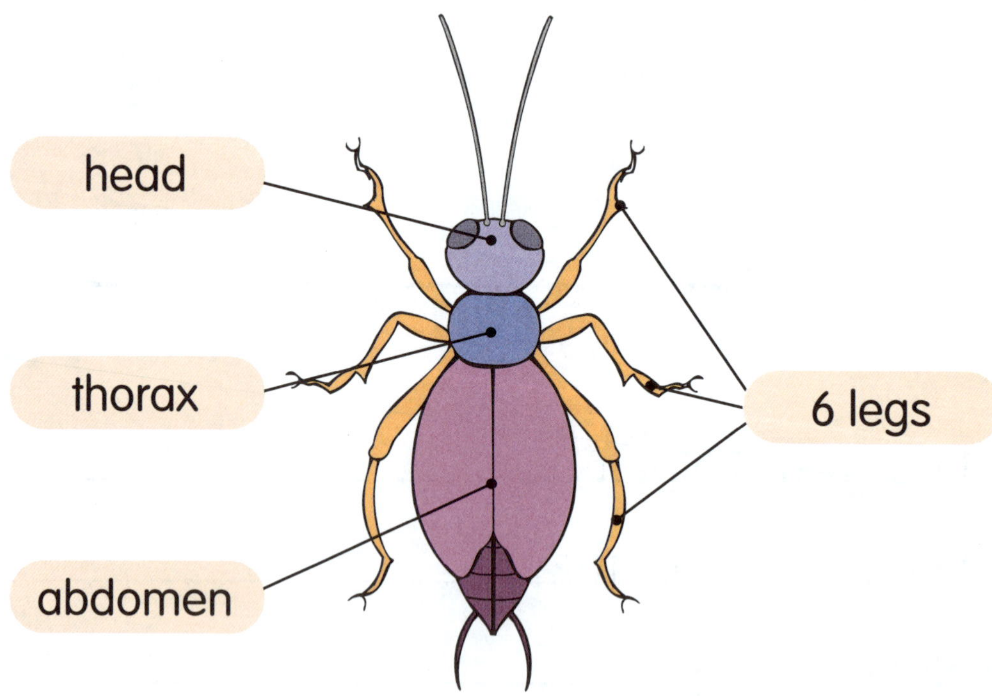

Insects look different from each other.

Insects move in different ways.

Some insects fly.

Some insects hop.

Some insects crawl.

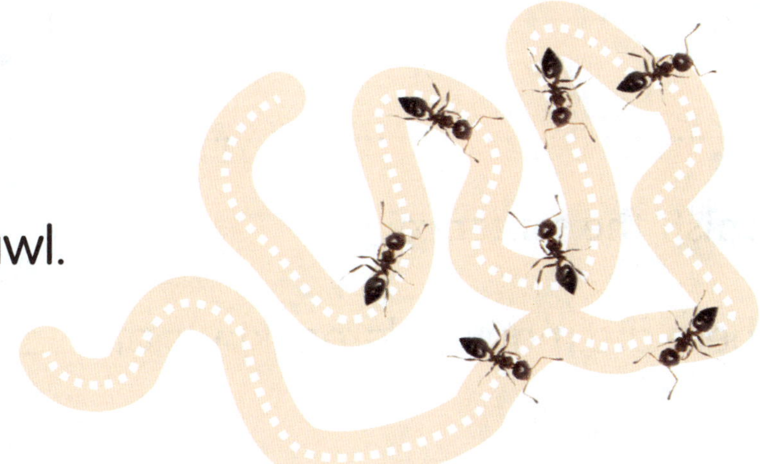

Skill:
Match graphic images to words

Insect Match

Draw a line to match.

butterfly

ant

bee

grasshopper

Finish the sentence.

There are many different kinds of ____________________.

Insects

Insect Parts

Trace the words.

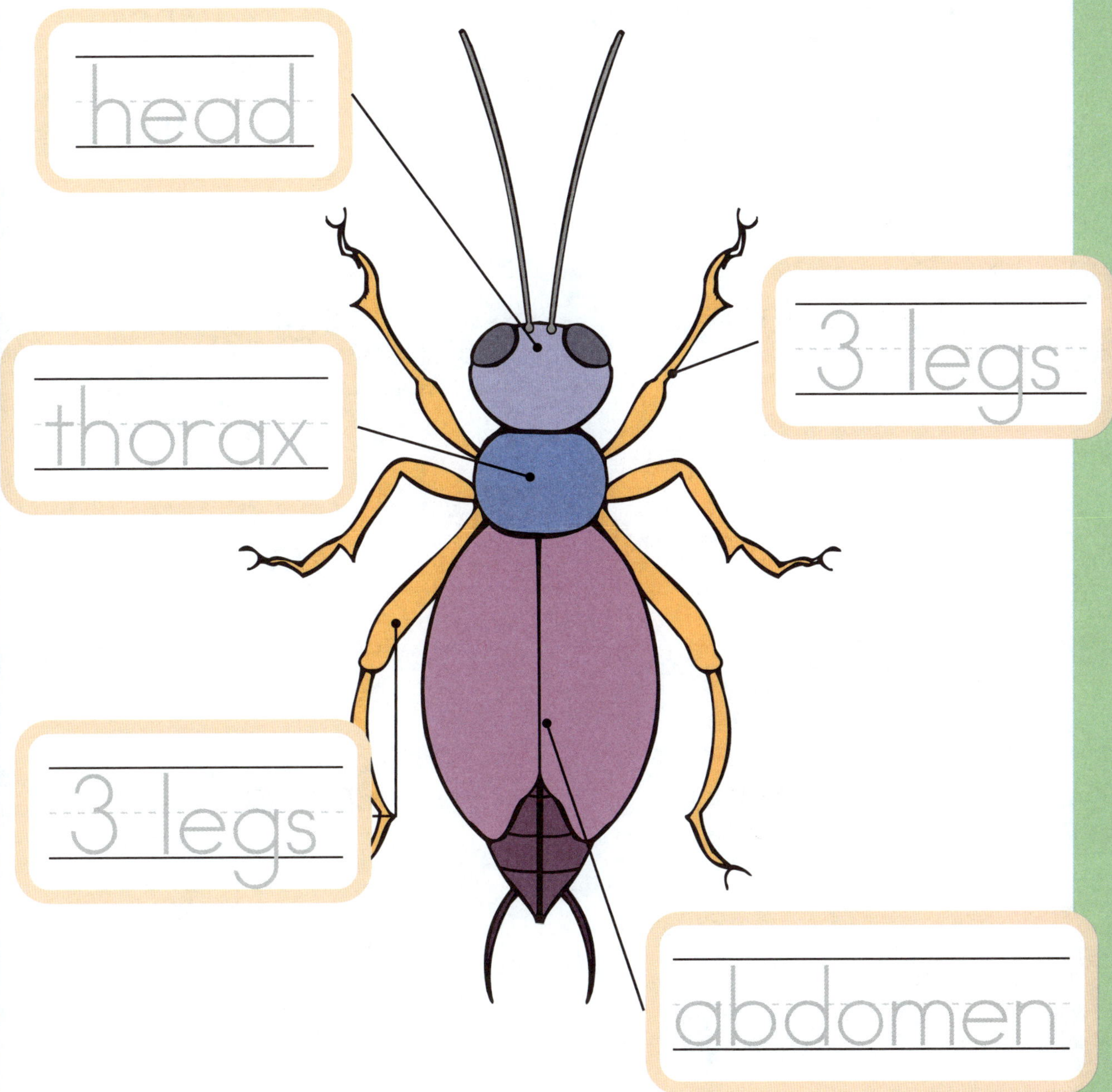

Skill:

Label graphic images to demonstrate understanding of science concepts

Insects

Skills:

Read science words; Visual discrimination

Insects

Insect Words

Unscramble the words about insects.
Write the words in the boxes.

Word Box

butterfly	moth	insect	wings
legs	body	ant	fly

thom ______	slge ______
lyf ______	tan ______
swnig ______	nestci ______
fylbertut ______	obyd ______

Use Vocabulary

Finish each sentence.

insects   butterflies   different

1. All ________________ have three body parts and six legs.

2. ________________ and moths are insects.

3. Insects may look ________________.

Draw an insect.

Skill:

Apply science vocabulary in context sentences

Insects

Skill:

Make real-world observations and write about them

Insect Hunt

Go outside and look for insects. Make a check mark for each insect you find.

ant ◯

fly ◯

bee ◯

moth ◯

butterfly ◯

ladybug ◯

Insect Book

Skill:

Make real-world observations and write about them

Make an insect book to read to someone.

What You Need

- 3 sheets of white paper
- 1 sheet of construction paper
- crayons, colored pencils, or markers
- stapler

What You Do

1. Think about the insects you saw on the insect hunt. Think about what each insect looks like and where you saw it.
2. Fold the sheets of paper and the construction paper in half. Staple the folded edge to make a book.
3. Cut out, from a magazine, a photo of an insect. Glue it to the cover of your book. Write a title for your book.
4. On each page of the book, draw a picture of a different insect and write a sentence about it.
5. After you are finished, read your book to someone.

Concept:

The moon and stars are objects in the sky.

The Night Sky

We see stars shining at night.
Stars make their own light.

We see the moon shining at night.
It does not make its own light.
Light from the sun makes
the moon shine bright.

Night Sky

The sun shines on the moon in different ways.

The part of the moon we can see changes.

We call these changes the phases of the moon.

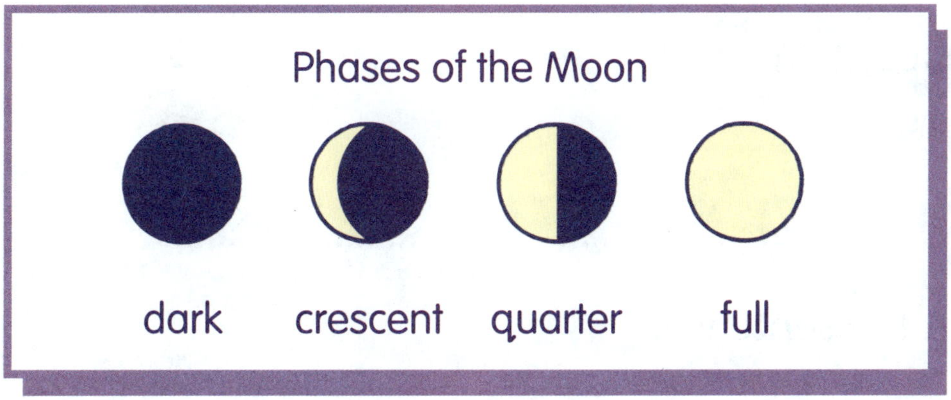

Skill:

Match graphic images to words

Night Sky

Objects in the Sky

Draw a line to match.

star

full moon

sun

crescent moon

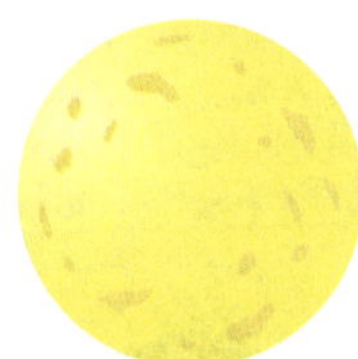

Finish the sentence.

The moon gets light from the ______________________.

Moon Phases

Skill:
Match graphic images to science concepts

Draw a line to match.

dark
cannot see the moon

quarter
can see half of the moon

full
can see all of the moon

crescent
can see a small part of the moon

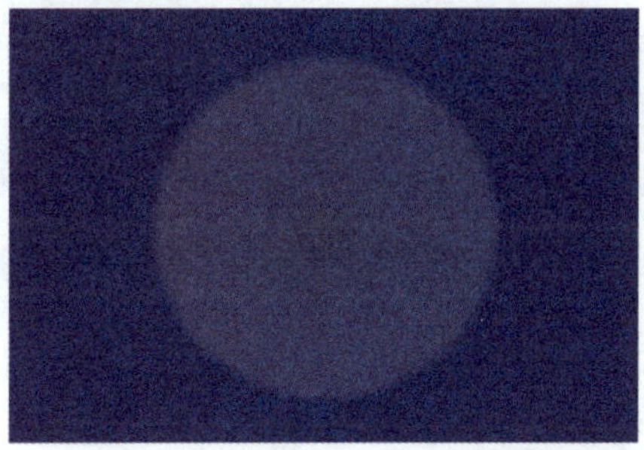

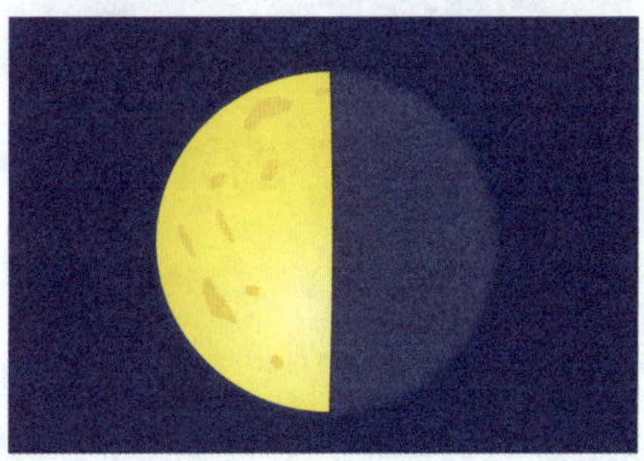

Skills:

Read science words; Visual discrimination

Night Sky Words

Unscramble the words about the night sky.
Write the words in the boxes.

Word Box

star	light	moon
sun	phases	shine

esshap ______

gilth ______

hisen ______

nus ______

omon ______

rast ______

Use Vocabulary

Skill:
Apply science vocabulary in context sentences

Finish each sentence.

moon	light	sun

1. Stars make their own ______________________.

2. Light from the ______________________ makes the moon shine bright.

3. The part of the ______________________ we can see changes.

Draw your favorite phase of the moon.

Skill:

Make art projects to represent science concepts

Moon Art

Make pictures that show the phases of the moon!

What You Need

- 3 sheets of white paper
- 3 sheets of black paper
- 4 sheets of colored construction paper
- a bowl or round traceable object
- crayons
- scissors
- glue

What You Do

1. Set a bowl on a white sheet of paper. Trace around it. Cut it out. Do the same thing with each sheet of white paper.
2. Repeat Step 1 with the three sheets of black paper.

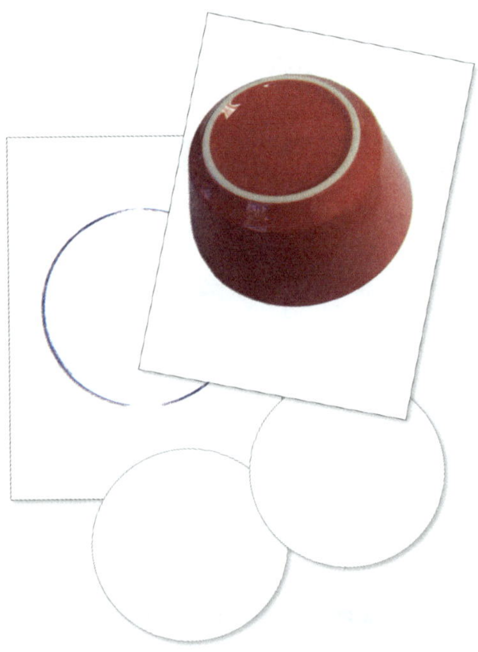

3. **Make a dark moon:** Glue a black circle to a piece of construction paper. Label it "dark moon."

4. **Make a crescent moon:** Cut a crescent shape out of a white circle. Glue it to a black circle. Glue it to the construction paper. Label it "crescent moon."

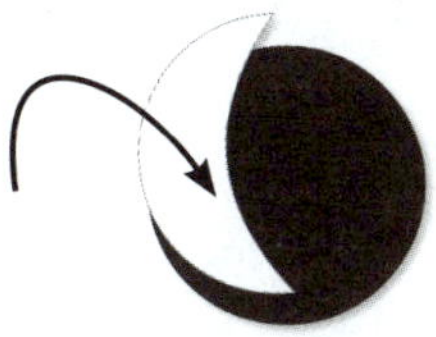

5. **Make a quarter moon:** Cut one black circle in half. Glue one half of it onto one full white circle. Glue it to the construction paper. Label it "quarter moon."

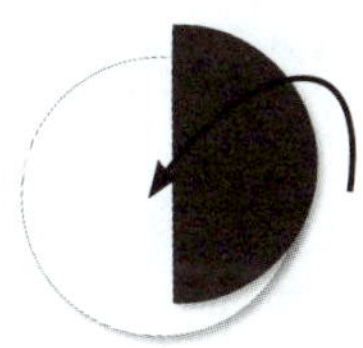

6. **Make a full moon:** Glue a white circle to a sheet of construction paper. Label it "full moon."

7. **Share it:** Put your pictures in order and tell someone about the phases of the moon.

Step 3 Step 4 Step 5 Step 6

Concept

People, plants, and animals need the sun's heat and light.

Our Sun

The sun is a star.
It is far, far away.

The sun is so hot
that we can feel its heat.

The sun is so bright
that we can see its light.

The sun warms the land, air, and water.

Sunlight warms the earth for people, animals, and plants to live.

Sunlight makes plants grow.

People and animals need plants for food.

Without the sun, nothing could live on Earth.

Our Sun

Skill:

Match graphic images to words

Sun Match

Draw a line to match.

sun

Earth

plants

animals

Finish the sentence.

The sun warms the land, air, and ______________________.

The Sun

Skill:
Match graphic images to words

Label the things that need the sun.

land   water   plants   animals   people

Skills:

Read science words; Visual discrimination

Our Sun

Sun Words

Read the words in the word box.
Find the hidden words. Circle them.

Word Box

heat	light	sun	earth
people	plants	animals	star

p	o	l	i	g	p	h	s	u	n
a	h	e	a	t	e	s	t	r	a
n	m	s	r	c	o	d	p	i	n
i	l	g	c	b	p	v	l	a	m
e	a	r	t	h	l	h	i	p	e
s	m	l	n	d	e	k	g	o	h
t	p	l	a	n	t	s	h	k	t
a	i	k	b	h	r	w	t	a	h
r	o	a	n	i	m	a	l	s	p

Use Vocabulary

Skill:
Apply science vocabulary in context sentences

Finish each sentence.

star	heat	warms

1. The sun is a ______________________.

2. The sun is so hot that we can feel its

   ______________________.

3. The sun ______________________ the land, air, and water.

Draw the sun warming people and animals.

Skill:

Make real-world observations and write about them

Hot Rocks

The sun warms the land. Test it for yourself!

What You Need

- 3 rocks of the same kind
- a black permanent marker

What You Do

1. Number each rock so that you will be able to identify it.
2. Set the numbered rocks in 3 different areas.

   Rock 1: a shaded spot indoors

   Rock 2: a shaded spot outdoors

   Rock 3: a sunny spot outdoors
3. After one hour, feel each rock. Draw an X on the Heat Chart to tell how each rock felt.
4. Then answer the questions about the rocks.

Heat Chart

Make an X to tell how each rock felt.

	Cold	Warm	Hot
Rock 1 shaded indoors			
Rock 2 shaded outdoors			
Rock 3 sunny outdoors			

1. Which rock felt the hottest?

____

2. Why do you think that was?

____

3. Which rock was the coolest?

____

4. Why do you think that was?

____

Concept:

Weather changes from season to season.

Seasons

Spring, summer, fall, and winter are seasons.

A season is a time of year.

Each season lasts three months.

The weather changes each season.

Spring can be warm and rainy.

Summer can be hot and sunny.

Fall can be cool and windy.

Winter can be cold and snowy.

Then the pattern starts all over with spring!

Skill:

Match graphic images to words

Season Match

Draw a line to match.

winter

spring

summer

fall

Finish the sentence.

A season is a time of ______________________.

Seasons

Season Names

Label each season. Draw a picture to tell about the weather.

winter   spring   summer   fall

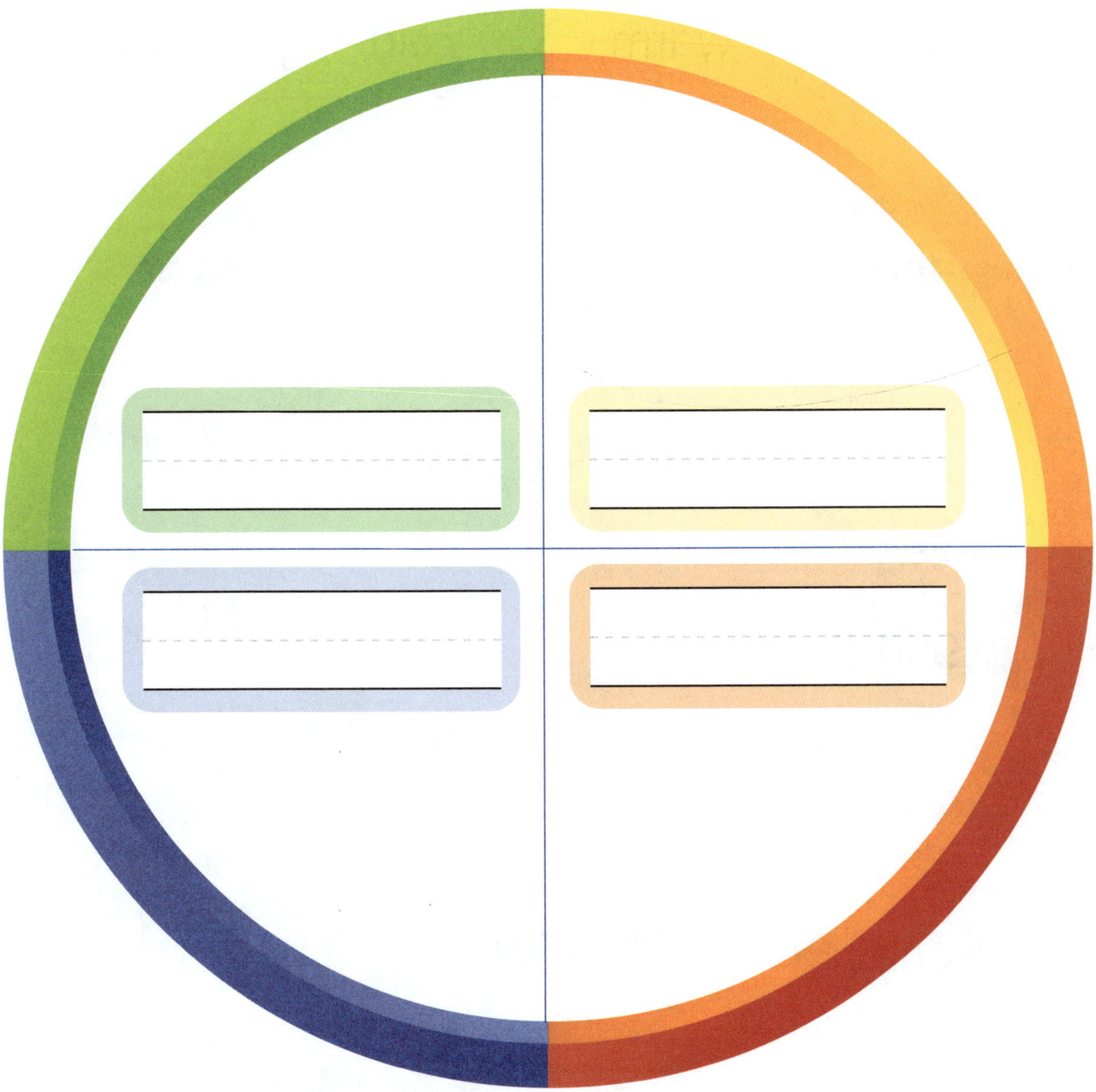

Skill:

Match graphic images to science concepts

Seasons

Skills:

Read science words; Visual discrimination

Season Words

Unscramble the words about the seasons.
Write the words in the boxes.

Word Box

summer	fall	spring	winter
season	warm	cold	hot

tho

mawr

dloc

grinsp

lafl

esonas

remsum

trinew

Use Vocabulary

Skill: Apply science vocabulary in context sentences

Finish each sentence.

weather   year   seasons

1. Spring, summer, winter, and fall are ________________.
2. A season is a time of ____________________.
3. The ____________________ changes each season.

Draw a picture of a tree in the fall.

Seasons

Skill:

Make art projects to represent science concepts

Seasons

Fingerpaint Trees

Use your hands to make trees for four seasons.

- white paper
- colored construction paper
- paints
- scissors
- glue
- paper plates

What You Do

1. Cut 2 sheets of white paper in half to make four sheets.
2. Pour brown paint onto a paper plate. Dip your hand and your wrist into the paint and press your hand and wrist onto one sheet of white paper to make the tree trunk and branches.
3. Do the same thing on each sheet of white paper. Let your "trees" dry.
4. Pour small amounts of colored paints onto paper plates. Dip the tip of your finger into one color at a time and fingerpaint leaves on the trees for each season.
5. After your trees are dry, glue them to the construction paper in order of the seasons: spring, summer, fall, winter.
6. Write about your painting on the next page.

Write about the weather and how the tree changed during each season in your painting.

Spring

weather: ______________________________

tree: ______________________________

Summer

weather: ______________________________

tree: ______________________________

Fall

weather: ______________________________

tree: ______________________________

Winter

weather: ______________________________

tree: ______________________________

Concept:

Trees provide material for many products.

Uses of Wood

Wood Is Good

Trees give us wood. People use wood to build and make things.

We use things made from wood at home, at school, and around town.

Uses of Wood

Some things made
from wood are large,
some are small.

Some are used outdoors,
some are used indoors.

Some are for play, and
some are very important.

Even paper is made from wood!
We use wood every day.

Skill:

Match graphic images to words

Uses of Wood

Wood Match

Draw a line to match.

home

school

town

Finish the sentence.

We use wood to ______________________ things.

Which Is Wood?

Look at the items in each box.
Circle the one that is made from wood.

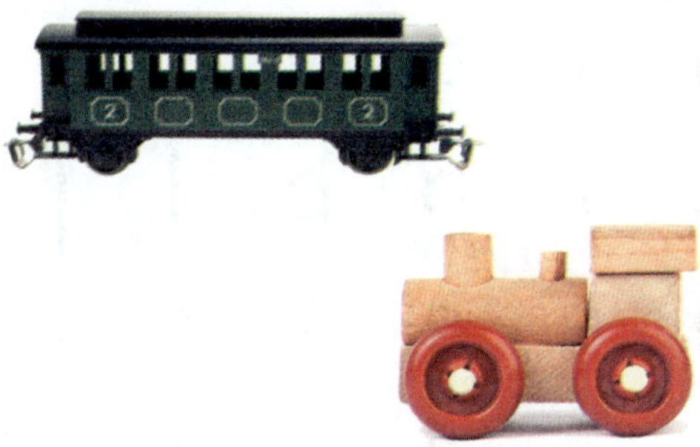

Skill:

Match graphic images to science concepts

Skills:

Read science words; Visual discrimination

Wood Words

Read the words in the word box.
Find the hidden words. Circle them.

Word Box

wood	build	trees	house
paper	school	town	table

m	s	c	h	o	o	l	e	e	o
r	c	t	r	e	a	c	c	t	w
p	a	p	e	r	h	t	b	a	t
w	d	w	c	p	a	r	h	b	l
b	h	o	u	s	e	e	s	l	c
u	n	d	w	o	r	e	n	e	m
i	h	t	v	k	b	s	d	c	l
l	e	w	o	o	d	a	i	m	r
d	r	i	n	c	t	o	w	n	e

Use Vocabulary

Skill:
Apply science vocabulary in context sentences

Finish each sentence.

town	trees	build

1. ____________________ give us wood.
2. People use wood to ____________________ things.
3. Many things around home, school, and ____________________ are made of wood.

Draw something that you use that's made from wood.

Skill:

Make real-world observations and write about them

Wood at Home

Look around your house and find things that are made from wood. Use the chart to show what the items are and how they are used.

1. Write the name of each item.

2. Draw a picture of the item.

3. Tell how you use the item.

Name of Item	What It Looks Like	How We Use It
pencil		To write with

I Use Wood to Make Things

Use wooden craft sticks to build something with wood.

Skill: Make art projects to represent science concepts

What You Need

- wooden craft sticks
- paper and pencil
- glue
- paint (optional)

What You Do

1. Think of something you'd like to build with the craft sticks. Some ideas are a pencil or toothbrush holder, an ornament, or a napkin holder.
2. Draw a picture of what you'd like to make.
3. Use craft sticks and glue to make your item.
4. If you use natural colored sticks, you may want to paint your item.
5. After it dries, use it!

Concept:
Earth has natural resources.

Earth Materials

We Use Materials

Earth has rocks, soil, and water. These are called earth materials. People, plants, and animals use earth materials to live.

Rocks have many different colors, sizes, and shapes. Some animals make their homes in rocks. People use rocks to build homes and buildings.

Soil has many different forms. Plants need soil to grow. Some animals need soil to build their homes.

Water is found in many places on Earth. People, plants, and animals need water to live. People use water to cook, clean, and do work.

Skill:

Match graphic images to words

Earth Materials

Earth Materials Match

Draw a line to match.

rocks

water

soil

Finish the sentence.

Soil, rocks, and water are called ____________________.

What Is It?

Skill:

Match graphic images to science concepts

Make an X on the one that doesn't belong.

rocks

water

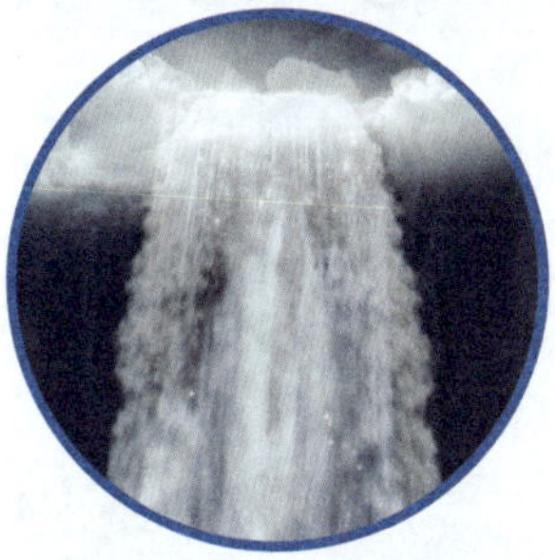

soil

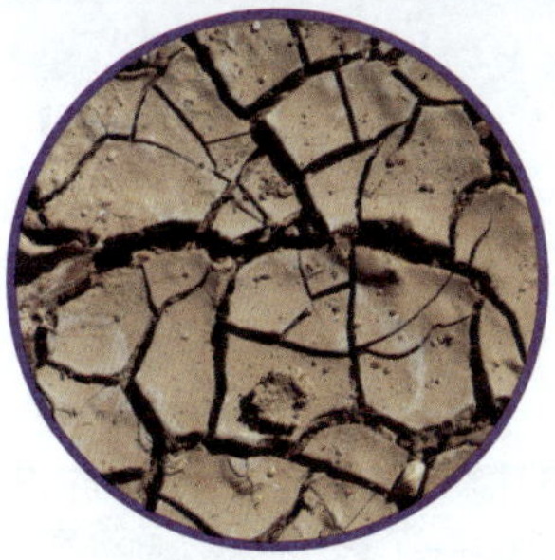

Earth Materials

Skills:

Read science words; Visual discrimination

Earth Materials Words

Read the words in the word box.
Find the hidden words. Circle them.

Word Box

water	soil	rock	plants
people	live	earth	materials

e m a t e r i a l s
a r w r o c k t h k
l w i v r s o i l p
p a h t p o r e k i
e t t v l e a r t h
o e w b a c m i c t
p r c h n a t w a l
l v r a t o l i v e
e i w c s m r a h i

Use Vocabulary

Skill:

Apply science vocabulary in context sentences

Finish each sentence.

live	rocks	materials

1. Earth has soil, ____________________, and water.
2. These are called earth ____________________.
3. People, plants, and animals use earth materials to ____________________.

Draw an earth material you use.

Skill:

Draw pictures to represent science concepts

Earth Materials

How I Use Earth Materials

Look around your house, both indoors and outdoors, and find earth materials you use.

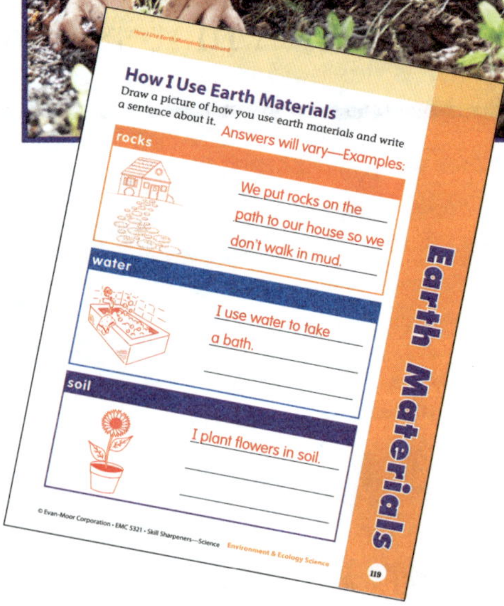

What You Do

1. Think about how you use these earth materials to help you do something.
2. Draw pictures and write about how you use each earth material on the next page.

How I Use Earth Materials

Draw a picture of how you use earth materials and write a sentence about it.

rocks

____

____

____

water

____

____

____

soil

____

____

____

Concept:

Recycling can reduce our impact on the environment.

Recycle and Reuse

Have you seen this?

It is on trash cans.

It is on bottles and cans.

It tells us to recycle or reuse.

We can recycle many things.

glass

plastic

paper

Some things are not easy to recycle. But you don't have to throw them away. You can reuse them in a different way.

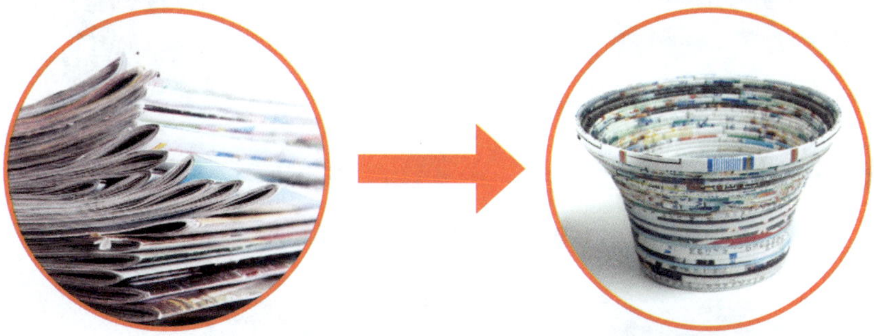

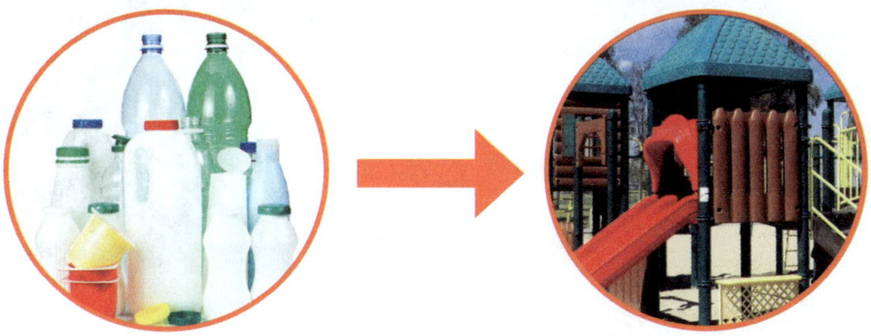

When we recycle or reuse things, we have less garbage. Having less garbage is good for Earth.

Skill:

Match graphic images to words

Recycling

Recycle Match

Draw a line to match.

plastic

glass

paper

recycle

Finish the sentence.

This  means ______________________.

Things to Recycle

Draw a line to match. Put the materials in the correct recycle bin!

Skill:

Match graphic images to science concepts

Recycling

Skills:

Read science words; Visual discrimination

Recycling

Recycling Words

Unscramble the words about recycling.
Write the words in the boxes.

Word Box

recycle	reuse	garbage	cans
earth	glass	paper	plastic

Use Vocabulary

Finish each sentence.

different recycle garbage

1. We can ________________________ many things.
2. We can reuse things in ________________________ ways.
3. When we recycle or reuse things, we have less ________________________.

Draw things you recycle.

Skill:

Apply science vocabulary in context sentences

Skill:

Make art projects to represent science concepts

Recycling

Birdfeeder

Reuse a milk carton to feed the birds in your backyard!

What You Need

- half-gallon (2 L) milk carton
- knife (adult use only)
- hole punch
- paint
- paintbrush
- 5 or 6 thin sticks (twigs or chopsticks)
- glue
- stickers, buttons, or beads
- birdseed

What You Do

1. Rinse out the milk carton well. Dry it. Set the milk carton on a flat surface.
2. Ask an adult to cut out an opening in one side of the carton as shown.
3. Punch a hole below the opening.

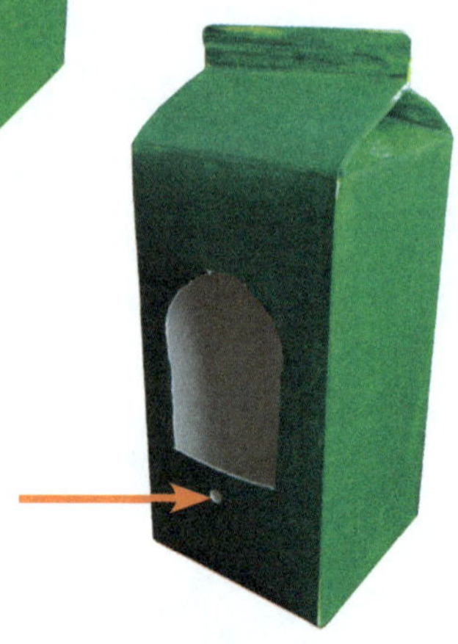

4. Paint the outside of the carton. After the paint dries, decorate the carton so it looks like it has flowers on it. Use stickers or glue buttons or beads onto it.
5. Ask an adult to cut the thin sticks into halves. Glue the sticks along both topsides of the carton to create a roof.
6. Place a long stick through the hole to make a perch. Glue the end of the stick to the inside back of the carton.
7. Fill the feeder with birdseed and place it outside.
8. Watch the birds use your reused milk carton as a feeder!

Concept:

The shape and design of a tool are related to its function.

The Best Tool for the Job

A tool is an item we use to do a job. Tools have different shapes to help us do different jobs.

Straws help us sip.

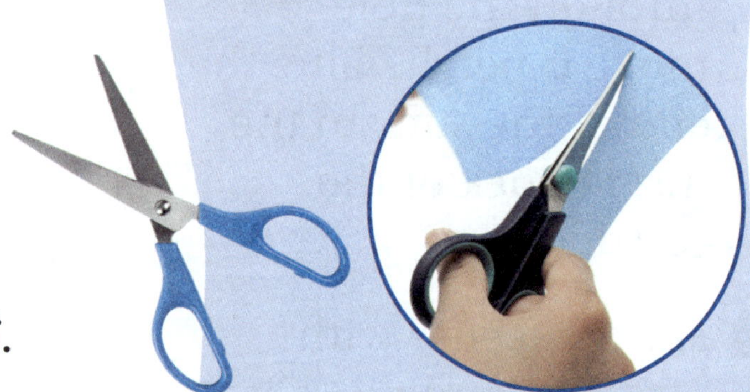

Scissors help us cut.

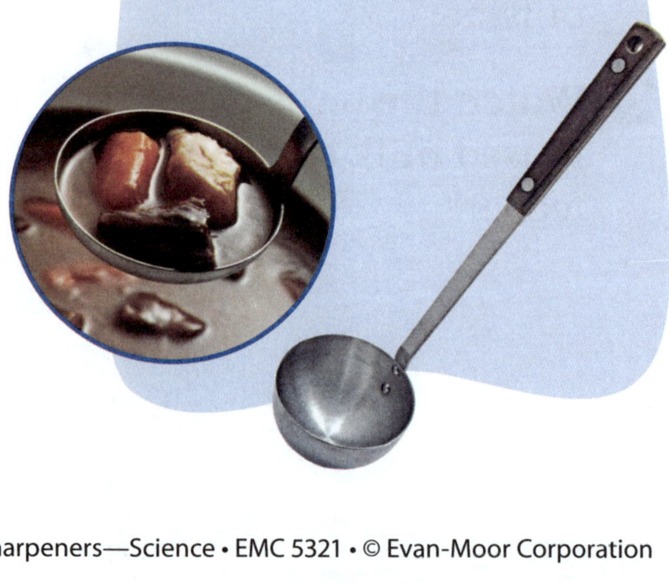

Ladles help us scoop.

Tools

Shovels help us dig.

Funnels help us pour.

Look around your house.
Notice the tools you use and how their special shapes help you do different jobs.

Skill:
Match graphic images to words

Tool Match

Draw a line to match.

scissors	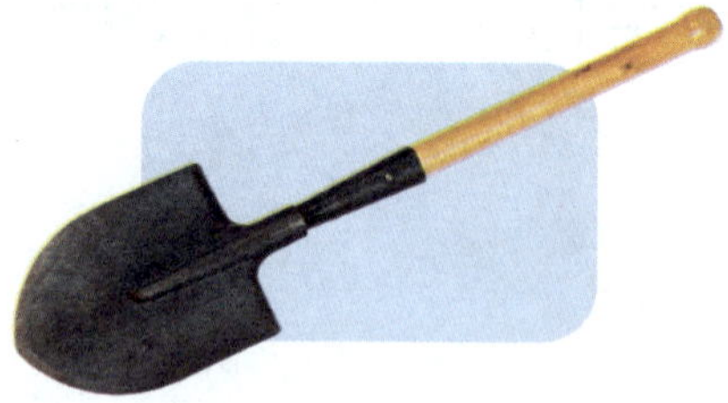
shovel	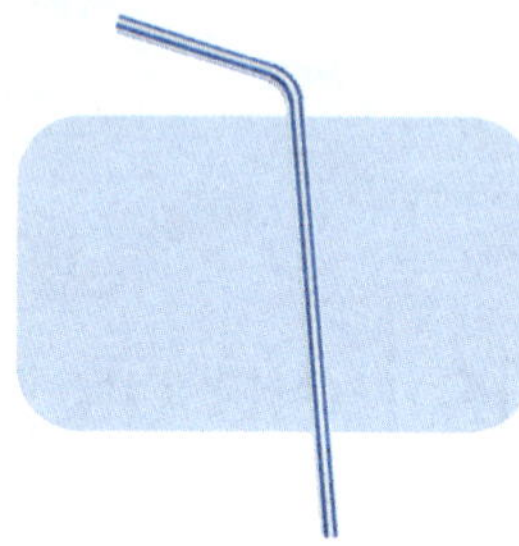
ladle	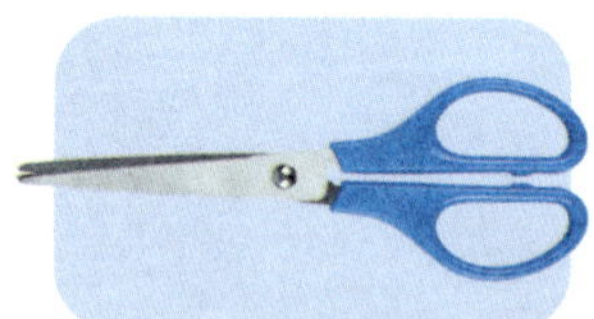
straw	

Finish the sentence.

The shape of each tool helps it do its ____________.

The Best Tool for the Job

Circle the tool that would be best for each job.

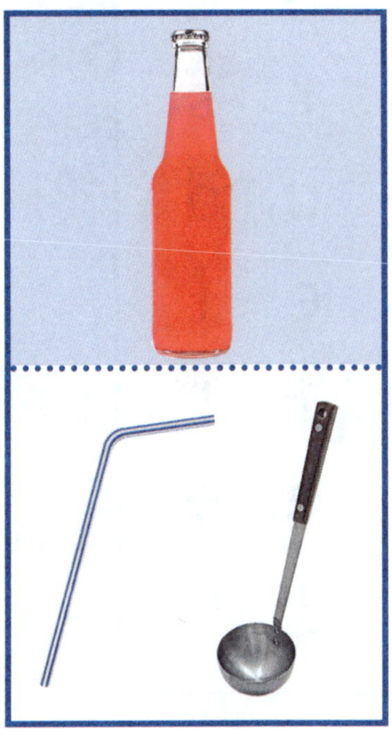

Skill:

Match graphic images to science concepts

Tools

Skills:

Read science words; Visual discrimination

Tool Words

Read the words in the word box.
Find the hidden words. Circle them.

Word Box

tool	shape	job	different
straw	scissors	shovel	ladle

o d i n s h o l r p
u i j o b b f f a r
h f s t n s h a p e
t f s c i s s o r s
o e c s o d i b a d
o r t t s h o v e l
l e c r s y a h f r
h n d a l a d l e e
a t h w a p e f j o

Use Vocabulary

Skill: Apply science vocabulary in context sentences

Finish each sentence.

tool	helps	shape

1. A ________________ is an item you use to do a job.
2. Each tool ________________ you do different things.
3. The ________________ of each tool helps it do its job.

Draw a picture of a tool that you use every day.

Skill:
Make projects to represent science concepts

Paper Funnel Tool

Make a paper funnel and try it out!

What You Need

- 1 sheet of paper (any kind)
- scissors
- tape

What You Do

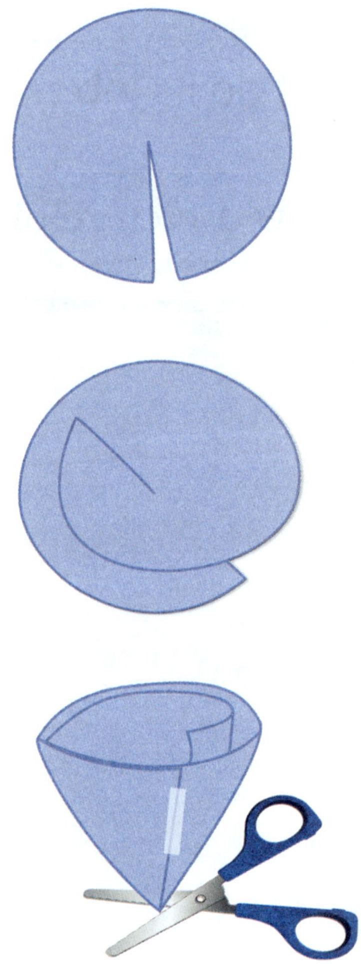

1. Cut a circle shape out of a piece of paper. It does not have to be a perfect circle.
2. From the outside edge, cut a slit to the center of the circle.
3. Slide one of the cut edges over the other. Continue to slide each of the cut edges opposite one another. Tape the outside edge so that it keeps its shape.
4. Cut the tip to create an opening. The size of the opening depends on what you will be funneling through it.

Tools

I Made a Tool

Tell about the paper funnel you made and how you used it.

I made a ________________________________.

I used it to ________________________________

____.

The ____________________ made work easier because

it helped me ________________________________

____.

Draw what you poured into your funnel, and the container that you poured it into.

This is how I used my paper funnel.

Answer Key

Page 10

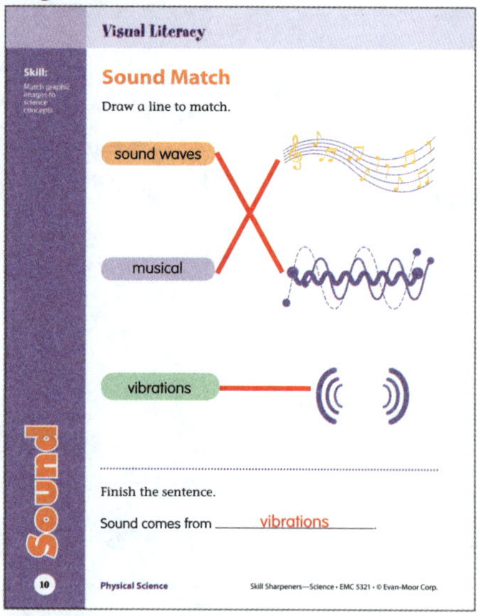

Visual Literacy

Skill: Match graphic images to science concepts

Sound Match

Draw a line to match.

sound waves

musical

vibrations

Finish the sentence.

Sound comes from vibrations.

Sound

10 Physical Science Skill Sharpeners—Science • EMC 5321 • © Evan-Moor Corp.

Page 11

Visual Literacy

Skill: Match graphic images to words

Making Sound

Draw a line to match.

hit

pluck

blow

shake

Sound

© Evan-Moor Corp. • EMC 5321 • Skill Sharpeners—Science Physical Science 11

Page 12

Vocabulary

Skills: Read science words; visual discrimination

Sound Words

Read the words in the word box.
Find the hidden words. Circle them.

Word Box

pluck	hit	vibrations	musical
shake	blow	sound	move

v	i	b	r	a	t	i	o	n	s
b	l	a	m	v	r	c	h	p	w
x	m	u	s	i	c	a	l	l	v
h	v	d	c	t	s	o	u	u	a
i	a	s	h	a	k	e	a	c	e
t	m	o	o	l	c	e	v	k	s
u	o	s	e	b	n	n	l	p	o
d	v	v	i	b	l	o	w	e	u
m	e	c	r	k	e	v	l	t	n
b	a	i	o	n	w	i	v	a	d

Sound

12 Physical Science Skill Sharpeners—Science • EMC 5321 • © Evan-Moor Corp.

Page 13

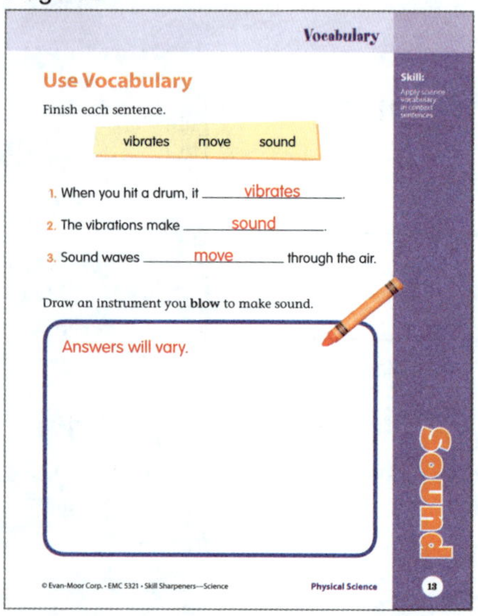

Vocabulary

Skill: Apply science vocabulary in context sentences

Use Vocabulary

Finish each sentence.

vibrates move sound

1. When you hit a drum, it vibrates.
2. The vibrations make sound.
3. Sound waves move through the air.

Draw an instrument you **blow** to make sound.

Answers will vary.

Sound

© Evan-Moor Corp. • EMC 5321 • Skill Sharpeners—Science Physical Science 13

Page 15

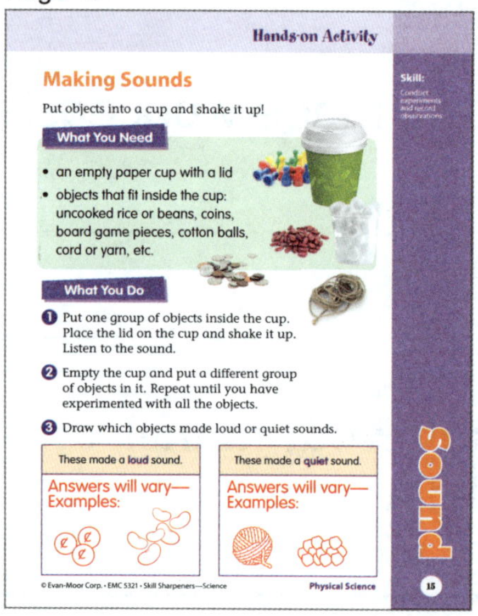

Hands-on Activity

Skill: Conduct experiments and record observations

Making Sounds

Put objects into a cup and shake it up!

What You Need

- an empty paper cup with a lid
- objects that fit inside the cup: uncooked rice or beans, coins, board game pieces, cotton balls, cord or yarn, etc.

What You Do

1. Put one group of objects inside the cup. Place the lid on the cup and shake it up. Listen to the sound.
2. Empty the cup and put a different group of objects in it. Repeat until you have experimented with all the objects.
3. Draw which objects made loud or quiet sounds.

These made a **loud** sound.	These made a **quiet** sound.
Answers will vary—Examples:	Answers will vary—Examples:

Sound

© Evan-Moor Corp. • EMC 5321 • Skill Sharpeners—Science Physical Science 15

Page 18

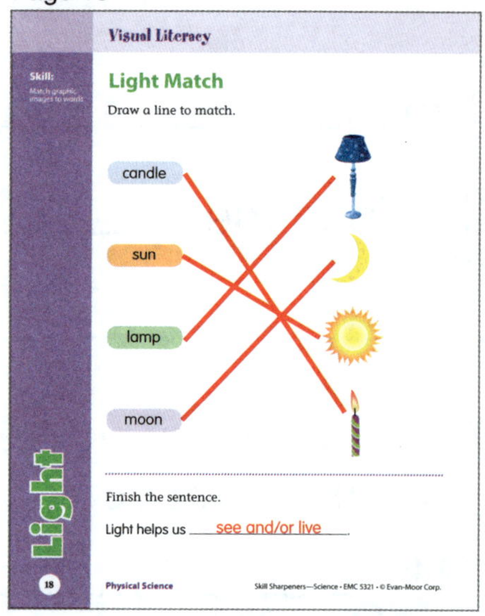

Visual Literacy

Skill: Match graphic images to words

Light Match

Draw a line to match.

candle

sun

lamp

moon

Finish the sentence.

Light helps us see and/or live.

Light

18 Physical Science Skill Sharpeners—Science • EMC 5321 • © Evan-Moor Corp.

Page 19

Visual Literacy

Skill: Match graphic images to science concepts

Who Makes It?

Look at the picture. Check the correct box.

nature people

nature ✓ people	nature people ✓
nature people ✓	nature ✓ people
nature people ✓	nature people ✓

Light

© Evan-Moor Corp. • EMC 5321 • Skill Sharpeners—Science Physical Science 19

Page 20

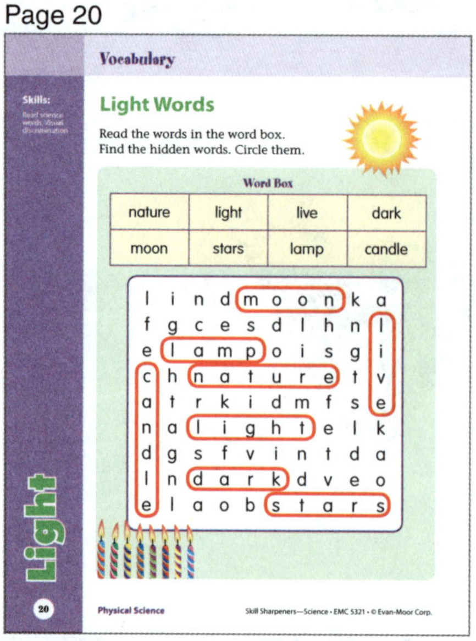

Vocabulary

Skills: Read science words; visual discrimination

Light Words

Read the words in the word box.
Find the hidden words. Circle them.

Word Box

nature	light	live	dark
moon	stars	lamp	candle

l	i	n	d	m	o	o	n	k	a
f	g	c	e	s	d	l	h	n	l
e	l	a	m	p	o	i	s	g	i
c	h	n	a	t	u	r	e	t	v
a	t	r	k	i	d	m	f	s	e
n	a	l	i	g	h	t	e	l	k
d	g	s	f	v	i	n	t	d	a
l	n	d	a	r	k	d	v	e	o
e	l	a	o	b	s	t	a	r	s

Light

20 Physical Science Skill Sharpeners—Science • EMC 5321 • © Evan-Moor Corp.

Page 21

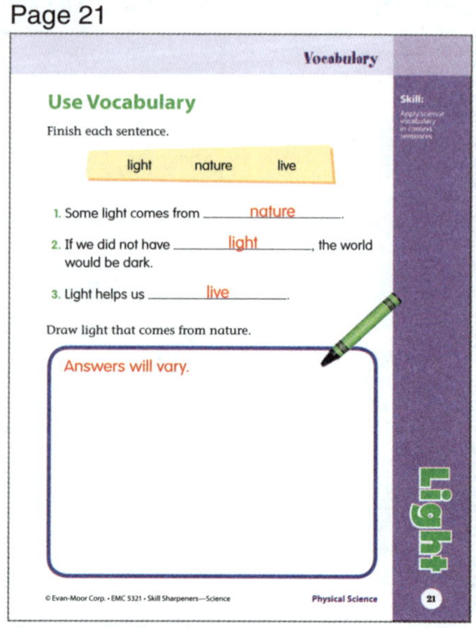

Vocabulary

Skill: Apply science vocabulary in context sentences

Use Vocabulary

Finish each sentence.

light nature live

1. Some light comes from nature.
2. If we did not have light, the world would be dark.
3. Light helps us live.

Draw light that comes from nature.

Answers will vary.

Light

© Evan-Moor Corp. • EMC 5321 • Skill Sharpeners—Science Physical Science 21

Page 22

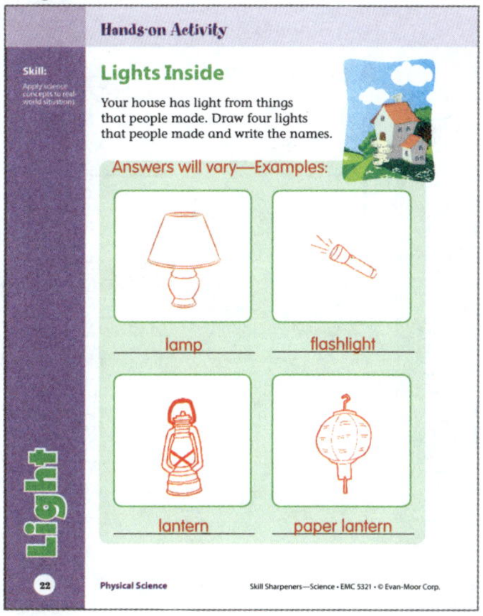

Hands-on Activity

Lights Inside

Skill: Apply science concepts to real-world situations

Your house has light from things that people made. Draw four lights that people made and write the names.

Answers will vary—Examples:

lamp

flashlight

lantern

paper lantern

Light

22 Physical Science Skill Sharpeners—Science • EMC 5321 • © Evan-Moor Corp.

Page 23

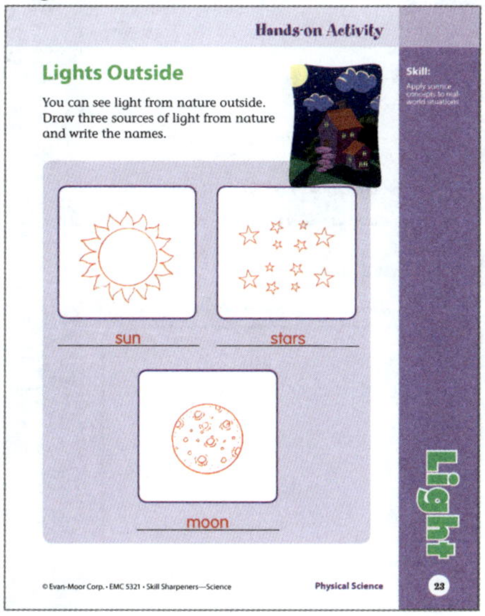

Hands-on Activity

Lights Outside

Skill: Apply science concepts to real-world situations

You can see light from nature outside. Draw three sources of light from nature and write the names.

sun

stars

moon

Light

© Evan-Moor Corp. • EMC 5321 • Skill Sharpeners—Science Physical Science 23

Page 26

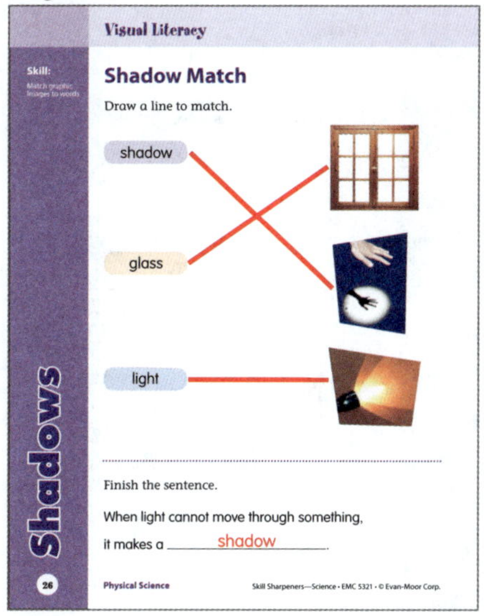

Visual Literacy

Shadow Match

Skill: Match graphic images to words

Draw a line to match.

shadow

glass

light

Finish the sentence.

When light cannot move through something, it makes a shadow.

Shadows

26 Physical Science Skill Sharpeners—Science • EMC 5321 • © Evan-Moor Corp.

Page 27

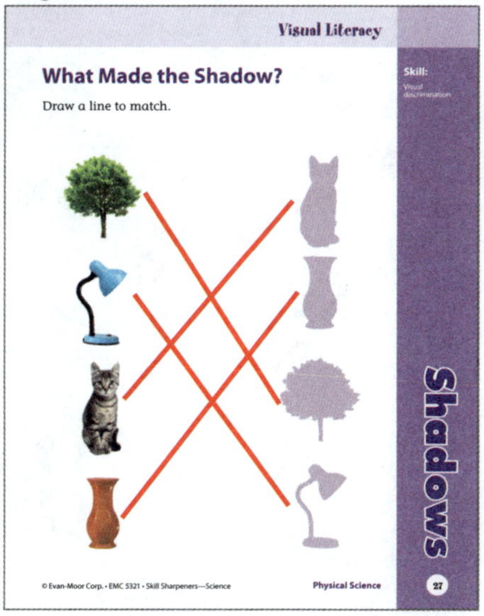

Visual Literacy

What Made the Shadow?

Skill: Visual discrimination

Draw a line to match.

Shadows

© Evan-Moor Corp. • EMC 5321 • Skill Sharpeners—Science Physical Science 27

Page 28

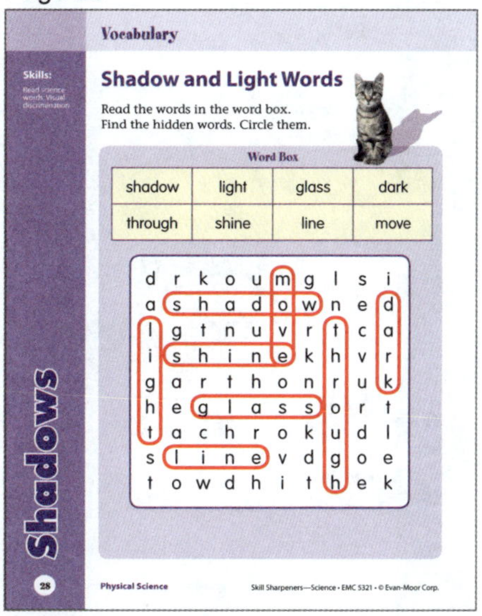

Vocabulary

Shadow and Light Words

Skills: Read science words; Visual discrimination

Read the words in the word box. Find the hidden words. Circle them.

Word Box

shadow	light	glass	dark
through	shine	line	move

d r k o u m g l s i
a s h a d o w n e d
l g t n u v r t c a
i s h i n e k h v r
g a r t h o n r u k
h e g l a s s o r t
t a c h r o k u d l
s l i n e v d g o e
t o w d h i t h e k

Shadows

28 Physical Science Skill Sharpeners—Science • EMC 5321 • © Evan-Moor Corp.

Page 29

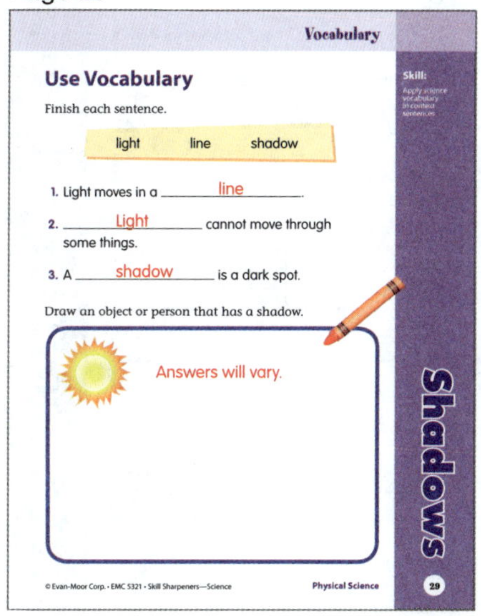

Vocabulary

Use Vocabulary

Skill: Apply science vocabulary in context sentences

Finish each sentence.

light line shadow

1. Light moves in a line.
2. Light cannot move through some things.
3. A shadow is a dark spot.

Draw an object or person that has a shadow.

Answers will vary.

Shadows

© Evan-Moor Corp. • EMC 5321 • Skill Sharpeners—Science Physical Science 29

Page 31

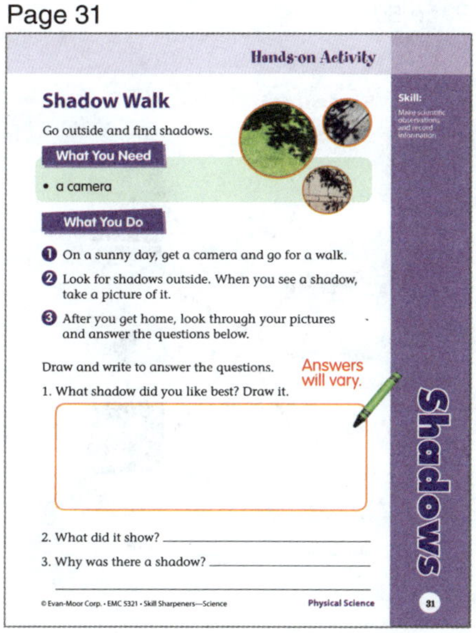

Hands-on Activity

Shadow Walk

Skill: Make scientific observations and record information

Go outside and find shadows.

What You Need

- a camera

What You Do

1. On a sunny day, get a camera and go for a walk.
2. Look for shadows outside. When you see a shadow, take a picture of it.
3. After you get home, look through your pictures and answer the questions below.

Draw and write to answer the questions. Answers will vary.

1. What shadow did you like best? Draw it.
2. What did it show?
3. Why was there a shadow?

Shadows

© Evan-Moor Corp. • EMC 5321 • Skill Sharpeners—Science Physical Science 31

Page 34

Visual Literacy

Tech Match

Skill: Match graphic images to words

Draw a line to match.

cellphone

computer

television

tablet

Finish the sentence.

These things are technology.

Technology

34 Physical Science Skill Sharpeners—Science • EMC 5321 • © Evan-Moor Corp.

Page 35

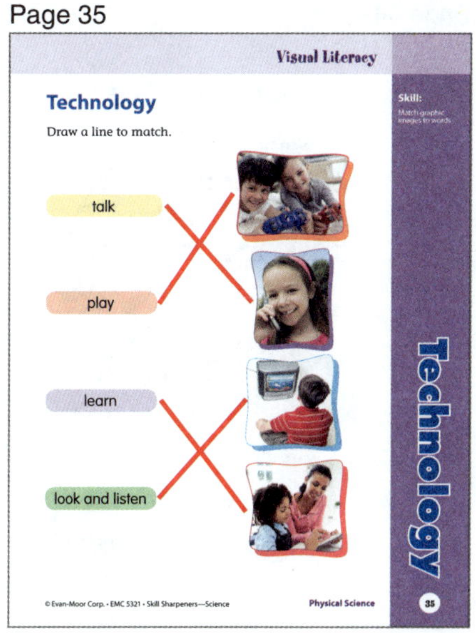

Visual Literacy

Technology

Skill: Match graphic images to words

Draw a line to match.

talk

play

learn

look and listen

Technology

© Evan-Moor Corp. • EMC 5321 • Skill Sharpeners—Science Physical Science 35

Page 36

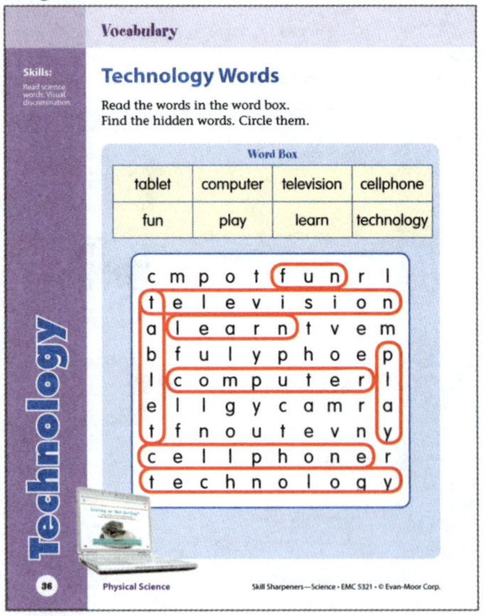

Vocabulary

Technology Words

Read the words in the word box.
Find the hidden words. Circle them.

Word Box

tablet	computer	television	cellphone
fun	play	learn	technology

c m p o t f u n r l
t e l e v i s i o n
a l e a r n t v e m
b f u l y p h o e p
l c o m p u t e r l
e l l g y c a m r a
t f n o u t e v n y
c e l l p h o n e r
t e c h n o l o g y

Technology

36 Physical Science Skill Sharpeners—Science • EMC 5321 • © Evan-Moor Corp.

Page 37

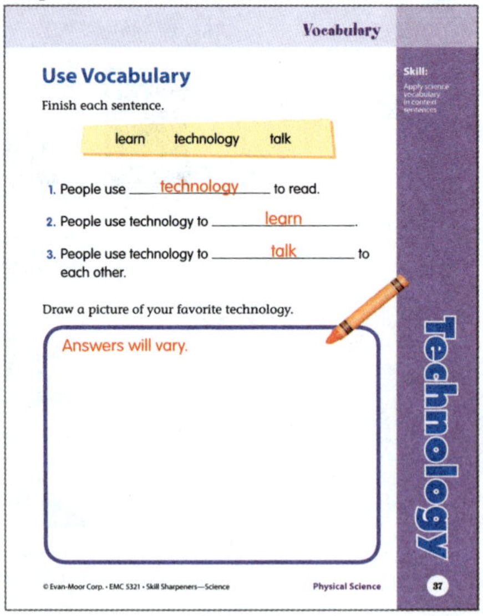

Vocabulary

Use Vocabulary

Finish each sentence.

learn technology talk

1. People use technology to read.
2. People use technology to learn.
3. People use technology to talk to each other.

Draw a picture of your favorite technology.

Answers will vary.

Technology

© Evan-Moor Corp. • EMC 5321 • Skill Sharpeners—Science Physical Science 37

Page 38

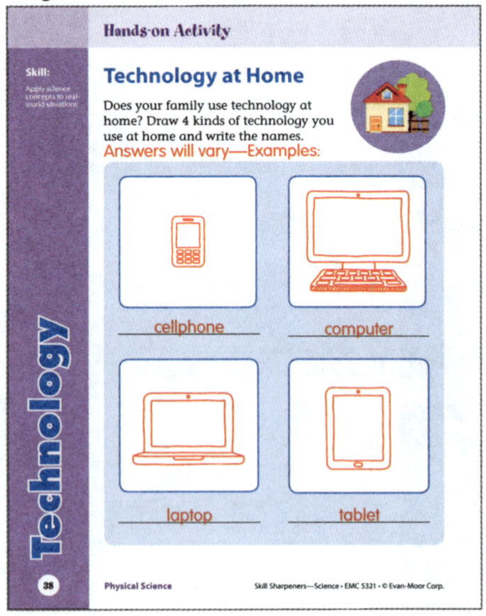

Hands-on Activity

Technology at Home

Does your family use technology at home? Draw 4 kinds of technology you use at home and write the names.
Answers will vary—Examples:

cellphone computer laptop tablet

Technology

38 Physical Science Skill Sharpeners—Science • EMC 5321 • © Evan-Moor Corp.

Page 39

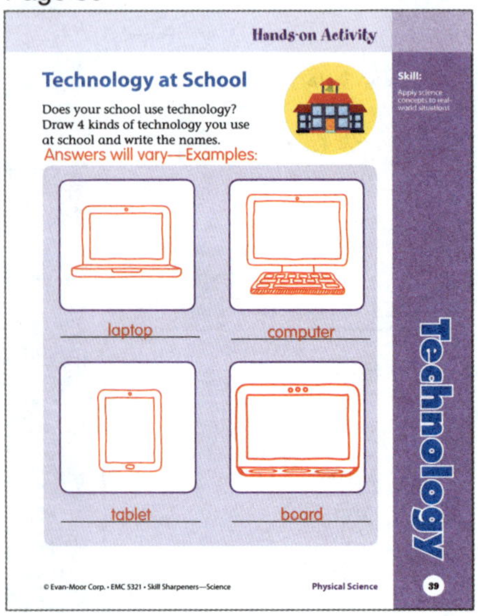

Hands-on Activity

Technology at School

Does your school use technology?
Draw 4 kinds of technology you use at school and write the names.
Answers will vary—Examples:

laptop computer tablet board

Technology

© Evan-Moor Corp. • EMC 5321 • Skill Sharpeners—Science Physical Science 39

Page 42

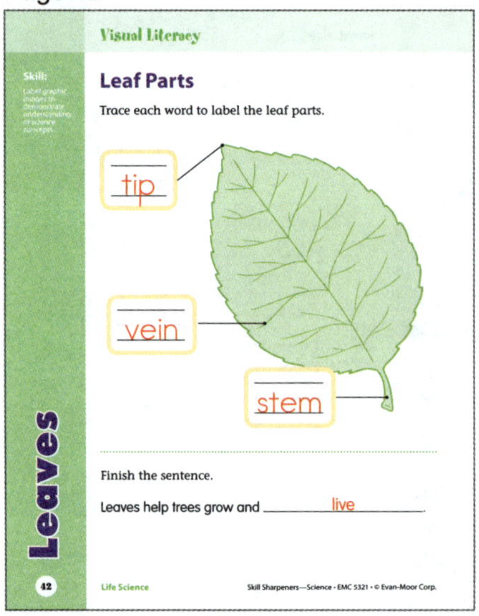

Visual Literacy

Leaf Parts

Trace each word to label the leaf parts.

tip vein stem

Finish the sentence.

Leaves help trees grow and live.

Leaves

42 Life Science Skill Sharpeners—Science • EMC 5321 • © Evan-Moor Corp.

Page 43

Visual Literacy

Leaves Have Shapes

Draw a line to match.

Leaves

© Evan-Moor Corp. • EMC 5321 • Skill Sharpeners—Science Life Science 43

Page 44

Vocabulary

Leaf Words

Unscramble the words about leaves.
Write the words in the boxes.

Word Box

tip	leaf	tree	sizes
leaves	live	shapes	grow

sevale leaves
fael leaf
eret tree
izsse sizes
ipt tip
viel live
phesas shapes
wogr grow

Leaves

44 Life Science Skill Sharpeners—Science • EMC 5321 • © Evan-Moor Corp.

Page 45

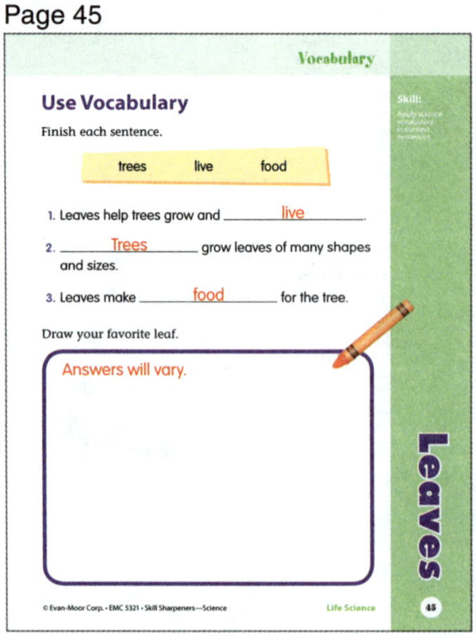

Vocabulary

Use Vocabulary

Finish each sentence.

trees live food

1. Leaves help trees grow and live.
2. Trees grow leaves of many shapes and sizes.
3. Leaves make food for the tree.

Draw your favorite leaf.

Answers will vary.

Leaves

© Evan-Moor Corp. • EMC 5321 • Skill Sharpeners—Science Life Science 45

Page 50

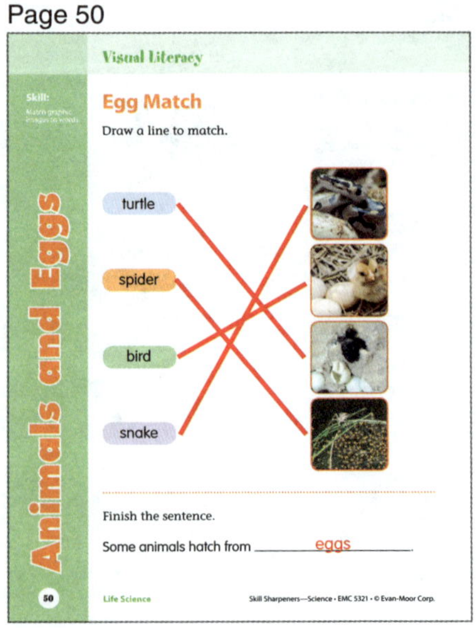

Visual Literacy

Egg Match

Draw a line to match.

turtle
spider
bird
snake

Finish the sentence.

Some animals hatch from eggs.

Animals and Eggs

50 Life Science Skill Sharpeners—Science • EMC 5321 • © Evan-Moor Corp.

Page 51

Visual Literacy

A Life Cycle

Number the pictures to match.

1. The egg is laid.
2. The egg hatches.
3. The baby is fed.
4. The baby is kept safe.

Answers: 2, 1, 4, 3

Skill: Label and/or sequence images to demonstrate understanding of science concepts

Animals and Eggs

© Evan-Moor Corp. • EMC 5321 • Skill Sharpeners—Science · Life Science · 51

Page 52

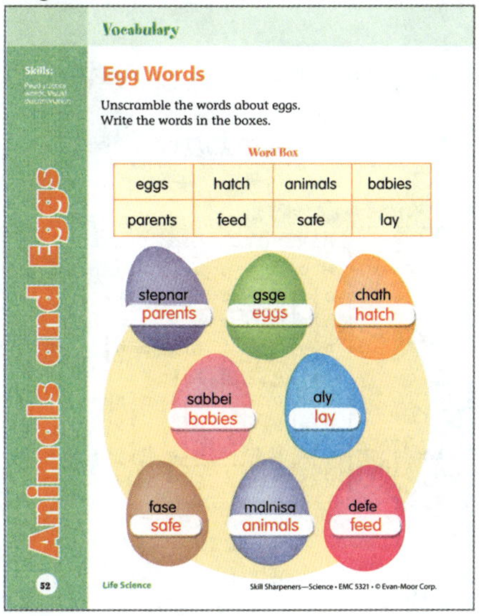

Vocabulary

Egg Words

Unscramble the words about eggs.
Write the words in the boxes.

Word Box

eggs	hatch	animals	babies
parents	feed	safe	lay

stepnar — parents
gsge — eggs
chath — hatch
sabbei — babies
aly — lay
fase — safe
malnisa — animals
defe — feed

Skills: Read science words; Visual discrimination

Animals and Eggs

52 · Life Science · Skill Sharpeners—Science • EMC 5321 • © Evan-Moor Corp.

Page 53

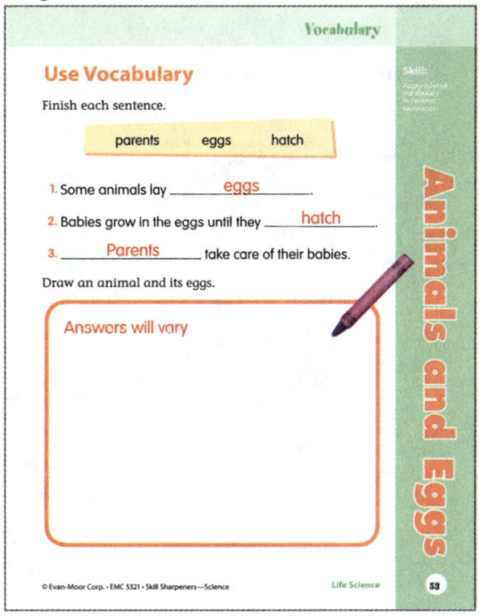

Vocabulary

Use Vocabulary

Finish each sentence.

parents eggs hatch

1. Some animals lay eggs.
2. Babies grow in the eggs until they hatch.
3. Parents take care of their babies.

Draw an animal and its eggs.

Answers will vary

Skill: Apply science vocabulary to complete sentences

Animals and Eggs

© Evan-Moor Corp. • EMC 5321 • Skill Sharpeners—Science · Life Science · 53

Page 58

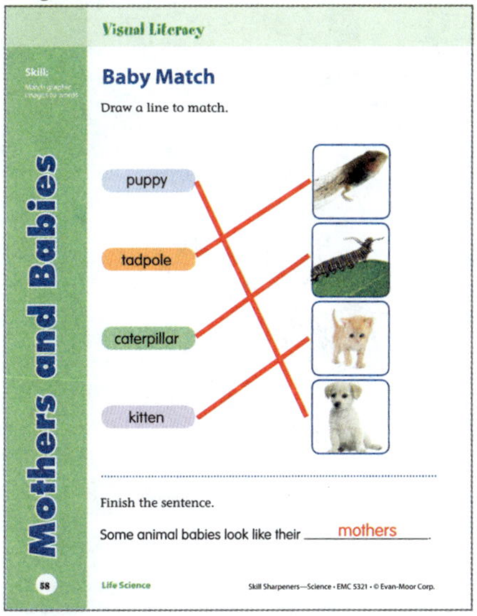

Visual Literacy

Baby Match

Draw a line to match.

puppy
tadpole
caterpillar
kitten

Finish the sentence.

Some animal babies look like their mothers.

Skill: Match graphic images to words

Mothers and Babies

58 · Life Science · Skill Sharpeners—Science • EMC 5321 • © Evan-Moor Corp.

Page 59

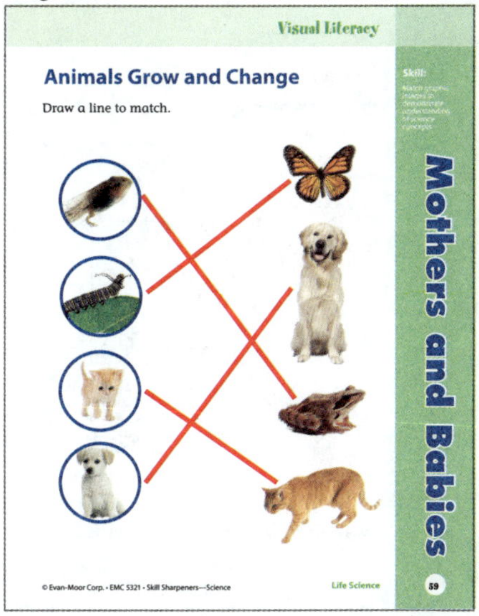

Visual Literacy

Animals Grow and Change

Draw a line to match.

Skill: Label and/or sequence images to demonstrate understanding of science concepts

Mothers and Babies

© Evan-Moor Corp. • EMC 5321 • Skill Sharpeners—Science · Life Science · 59

Page 60

Vocabulary

Mothers and Babies Words

Read the words in the word box.
Find the hidden words. Circle them.

Word Box

animal	babies	mothers	grow
change	born	butterfly	alike

c h a e t a r g l y
m f n b a b i e s e
o l i a b c g r o w
t a m o r i k e a l
h r a b r m o t n i
e g l u n c h a e m
r e y c h a l i k e
s b u t t e r f l y
c h a n g e b o r n

Skills: Read science words; Visual discrimination

Mothers and Babies

60 · Life Science · Skill Sharpeners—Science • EMC 5321 • © Evan-Moor Corp.

Page 61

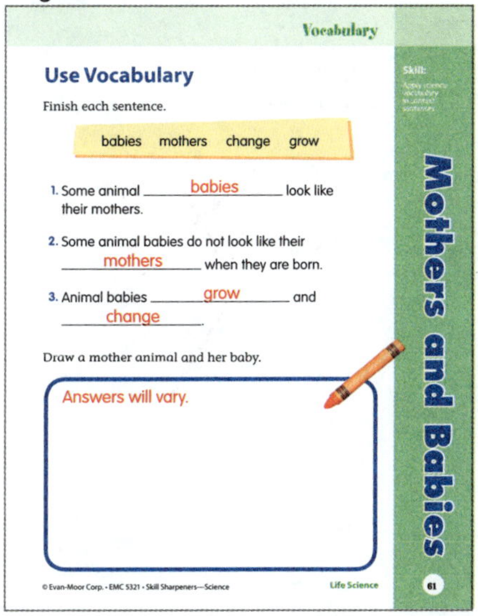

Vocabulary

Use Vocabulary

Finish each sentence.

babies mothers change grow

1. Some animal babies look like their mothers.
2. Some animal babies do not look like their mothers when they are born.
3. Animal babies grow and change.

Draw a mother animal and her baby.

Answers will vary.

Skill: Apply science vocabulary to complete sentences

Mothers and Babies

© Evan-Moor Corp. • EMC 5321 • Skill Sharpeners—Science · Life Science · 61

Page 63

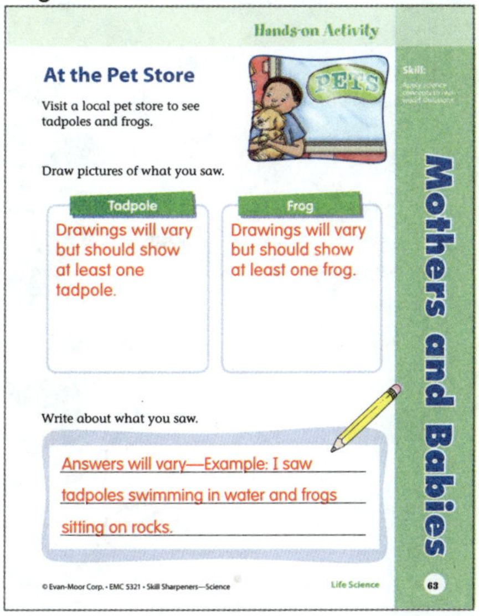

Hands-on Activity

At the Pet Store

Visit a local pet store to see tadpoles and frogs.

PETS

Draw pictures of what you saw.

Tadpole	Frog
Drawings will vary but should show at least one tadpole.	Drawings will vary but should show at least one frog.

Write about what you saw.

Answers will vary—Example: I saw tadpoles swimming in water and frogs sitting on rocks.

Skill: Apply science concepts to real-world situations

Mothers and Babies

© Evan-Moor Corp. • EMC 5321 • Skill Sharpeners—Science · Life Science · 63

Page 66

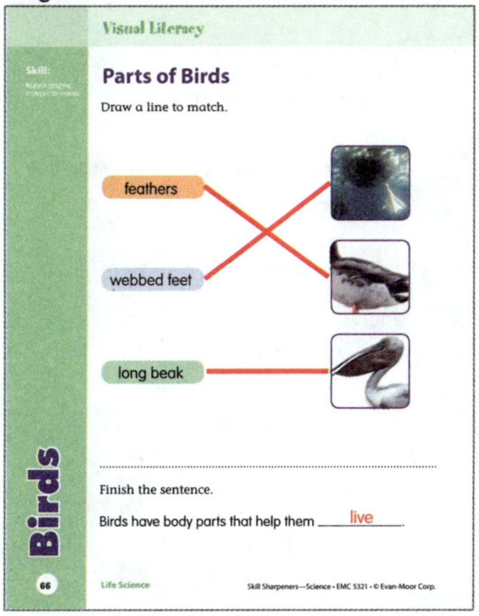

Visual Literacy

Parts of Birds

Draw a line to match.

feathers
webbed feet
long beak

Finish the sentence.

Birds have body parts that help them live.

Skill: Match graphic images to words

Birds

66 · Life Science · Skill Sharpeners—Science • EMC 5321 • © Evan-Moor Corp.

Page 67

Visual Literacy

Different Types of Beaks

Read the chart.

Skill: Interpret information from charts or graphs

Type of Beak	What It Looks Like	What It's Used For
Spear beak		stabbing fish
Scoop beak		scooping fish out of water
Cracker beak		cracking seeds open

1. Which beak is used for scooping fish out of water? scoop beak
2. Which beak is used for cracking seeds? cracker beak

Birds

© Evan-Moor Corp. • EMC 5321 • Skill Sharpeners—Science · Life Science · 67

Page 68

Vocabulary

Bird Words

Skills: Read science words; Use visual discrimination

Read the words in the word box.
Find the hidden words. Circle them.

Word Box

birds	feathers	webbed	beaks
feet	swim	body	parts

w e b e a k s w e n
e f c h d a r p t s
h e m w e b b e d w
n a f e t r p o b i
d t b o d y a k f m
b h o y b b r a e t
b e s i f a t r e i
e r w m e h s b t r
p s e b i r d s o d

Birds

68 · Life Science · Skill Sharpeners—Science • EMC 5321 • © Evan-Moor Corp.

Page 69

Vocabulary

Use Vocabulary

Skill: Apply science vocabulary in written sentences

Finish each sentence.

webbed feet · feathers · shape

1. Birds have feathers to keep them warm and dry.
2. Some birds have webbed feet.
3. The shape of a bird's beak helps it eat.

Draw a bird using its beak to eat.

Answers will vary.

Birds

© Evan-Moor Corp. • EMC 5321 • Skill Sharpeners—Science · Life Science · 69

Page 71

Bird Facts, continued

Answers will vary.

bird's name

This bird's beak helps it ______

This bird's wings help it ______

This bird's feet help it ______

Birds

© Evan-Moor Corp. • EMC 5321 • Skill Sharpeners—Science · Life Science · 71

Page 74

Visual Literacy

Insect Match

Skill: Match graphic images to words

Draw a line to match.

butterfly · ant · bee · grasshopper

Finish the sentence.

There are many different kinds of insects.

Insects

74 · Life Science · Skill Sharpeners—Science • EMC 5321 • © Evan-Moor Corp.

Page 75

Visual Literacy

Insect Parts

Skill: Label graphic images to demonstrate understanding of science concepts

Trace the words.

Insects

© Evan-Moor Corp. • EMC 5321 • Skill Sharpeners—Science · Life Science · 75

Page 76

Vocabulary

Insect Words

Skills: Read science words; Use visual discrimination

Unscramble the words about insects.
Write the words in the boxes.

Word Box

butterfly	moth	insect	wings
legs	body	ant	fly

Scrambled	Answer	Scrambled	Answer
thom	moth	slge	legs
lyf	fly	tan	ant
swnig	wings	nestci	insect
fylbertut	butterfly	obyd	body

Insects

76 · Life Science · Skill Sharpeners—Science • EMC 5321 • © Evan-Moor Corp.

Page 77

Vocabulary

Use Vocabulary

Skill: Apply science vocabulary in written sentences

Finish each sentence.

insects · butterflies · different

1. All insects have three body parts and six legs.
2. Butterflies and moths are insects.
3. Insects may look different.

Draw an insect.

Answers will vary.

Insects

© Evan-Moor Corp. • EMC 5321 • Skill Sharpeners—Science · Life Science · 77

Page 82

Visual Literacy

Objects in the Sky

Skill: Match graphic images to words

Draw a line to match.

star · full moon · sun · crescent moon

Finish the sentence.

The moon gets light from the sun.

Night Sky

82 · Space and Earth Science · Skill Sharpeners—Science • EMC 5321 • © Evan-Moor Corp.

Page 83

Moon Phases

Skill: Match graphic images to science concepts

Draw a line to match.

dark — cannot see the moon

quarter — can see half of the moon

full — can see all of the moon

crescent — can see a small part of the moon

Night Sky

Page 84

Night Sky Words

Skills: Read science words; Visual discrimination

Unscramble the words about the night sky.
Write the words in the boxes.

Word Box

star	light	moon
sun	phases	shine

esshap — phases

gilth — light

hisen — shine

nus — sun

omon — moon

rast — star

Night Sky

Page 85

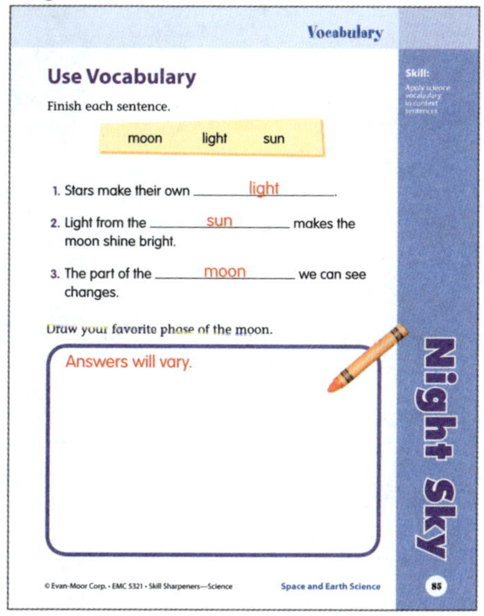

Use Vocabulary

Skill: Apply science vocabulary in context sentences

Finish each sentence.

moon light sun

1. Stars make their own light.
2. Light from the sun makes the moon shine bright.
3. The part of the moon we can see changes.

Draw your favorite phase of the moon.

Answers will vary.

Night Sky

Page 90

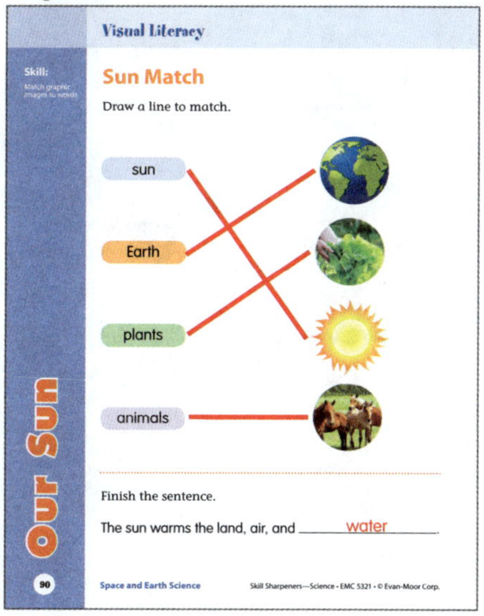

Sun Match

Skill: Match graphic images to words

Draw a line to match.

sun

Earth

plants

animals

Finish the sentence.

The sun warms the land, air, and water.

Our Sun

Page 91

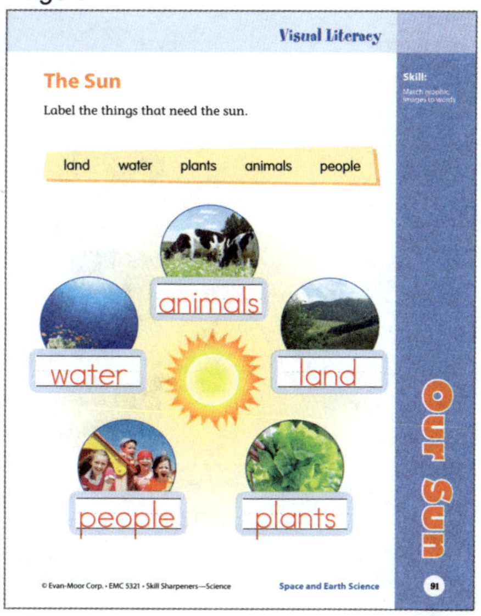

The Sun

Skill: Match graphic images to words

Label the things that need the sun.

land water plants animals people

animals

water

land

people

plants

Our Sun

Page 92

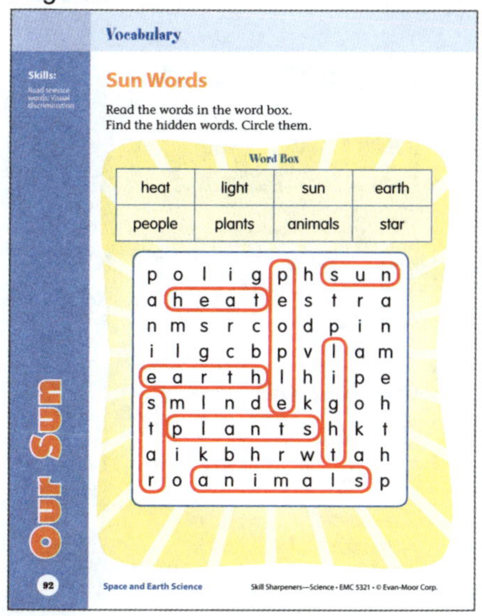

Sun Words

Skills: Read science words; Visual discrimination

Read the words in the word box.
Find the hidden words. Circle them.

Word Box

heat	light	sun	earth
people	plants	animals	star

p o l i g p h s u n
a h e a t e s t r a
n m s r c o d p i n
i l g c b p v l a m
e a r t h l h i p e
s m l n d e k g o h
t p l a n t s h k t
a i k b h r w t a h
r o a n i m a l s p

Our Sun

Page 93

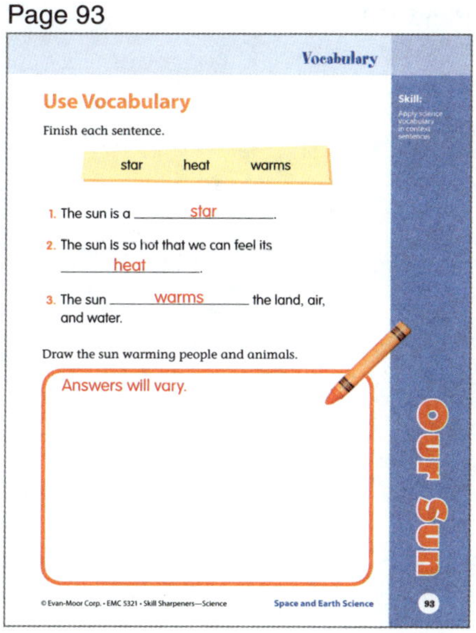

Use Vocabulary

Skill: Apply science vocabulary in context sentences

Finish each sentence.

star heat warms

1. The sun is a star.
2. The sun is so hot that we can feel its heat.
3. The sun warms the land, air, and water.

Draw the sun warming people and animals.

Answers will vary.

Our Sun

Page 95

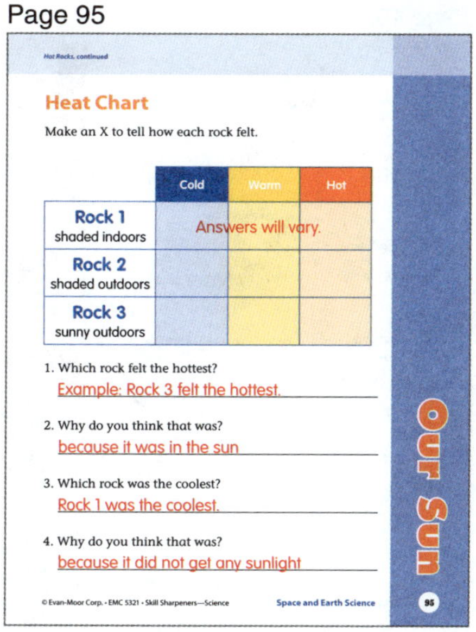

Heat Chart

Make an X to tell how each rock felt.

	Cold	Warm	Hot
Rock 1 shaded indoors	Answers will vary.		
Rock 2 shaded outdoors			
Rock 3 sunny outdoors			

1. Which rock felt the hottest?
   Example: Rock 3 felt the hottest.
2. Why do you think that was?
   because it was in the sun
3. Which rock was the coolest?
   Rock 1 was the coolest.
4. Why do you think that was?
   because it did not get any sunlight

Our Sun

Page 98

Season Match

Skill: Match graphic images to words

Draw a line to match.

winter

spring

summer

fall

Finish the sentence.

A season is a time of year.

Seasons

Page 99

Visual Literacy

Season Names

Label each season. Draw a picture to tell about the weather.

winter spring summer fall

Drawings will vary but should match season labels.

spring summer winter fall

Skill:

Seasons

© Evan-Moor Corp. • EMC 5321 • Skill Sharpeners—Science · Space and Earth Science · 99

Page 100

Vocabulary

Season Words

Unscramble the words about the seasons. Write the words in the boxes.

Word Box

summer	fall	spring	winter
season	warm	cold	hot

tho — hot
mawr — warm
dloc — cold
grinsp — spring
lafl — fall
esonas — season
remsum — summer
trinew — winter

Skills:

Seasons

100 · Space and Earth Science · Skill Sharpeners—Science • EMC 5321 • © Evan-Moor Corp.

Page 101

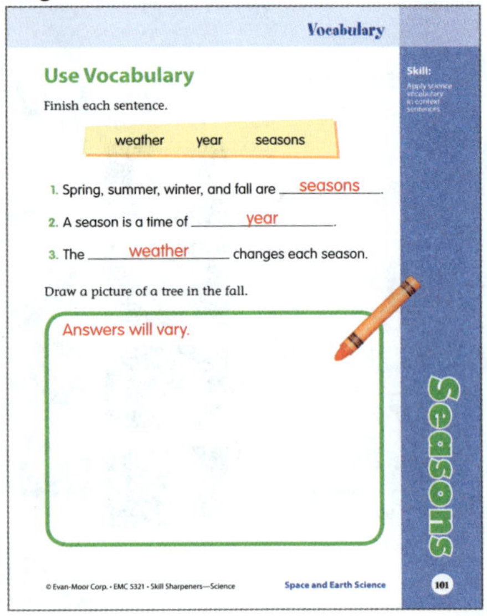
Vocabulary

Use Vocabulary

Finish each sentence.

weather year seasons

1. Spring, summer, winter, and fall are seasons.
2. A season is a time of year.
3. The weather changes each season.

Draw a picture of a tree in the fall.

Answers will vary.

Skill:

Seasons

© Evan-Moor Corp. • EMC 5321 • Skill Sharpeners—Science · Space and Earth Science · 101

Page 103

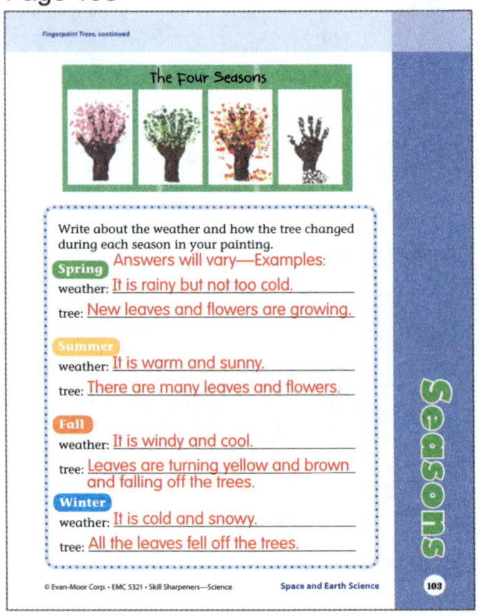
Fingerpaint Trees, continued

The Four Seasons

Write about the weather and how the tree changed during each season in your painting.

Answers will vary—Examples:

Spring
weather: It is rainy but not too cold.
tree: New leaves and flowers are growing.

Summer
weather: It is warm and sunny.
tree: There are many leaves and flowers.

Fall
weather: It is windy and cool.
tree: Leaves are turning yellow and brown and falling off the trees.

Winter
weather: It is cold and snowy.
tree: All the leaves fell off the trees.

Seasons

© Evan-Moor Corp. • EMC 5321 • Skill Sharpeners—Science · Space and Earth Science · 103

Page 106

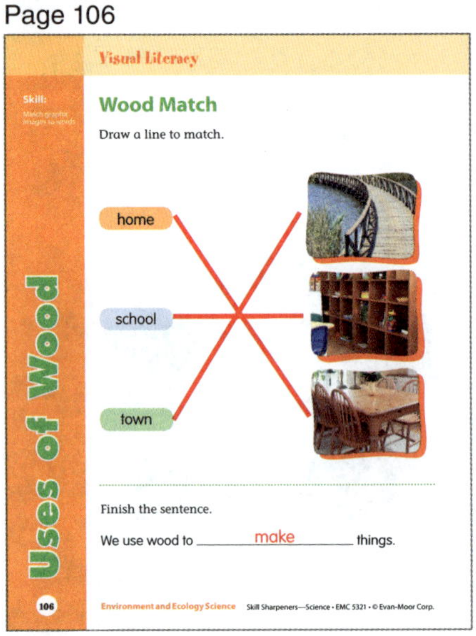
Visual Literacy

Wood Match

Draw a line to match.

home
school
town

Finish the sentence.

We use wood to make things.

Skill:

Uses of Wood

106 · Environment and Ecology Science · Skill Sharpeners—Science • EMC 5321 • © Evan-Moor Corp.

Page 107

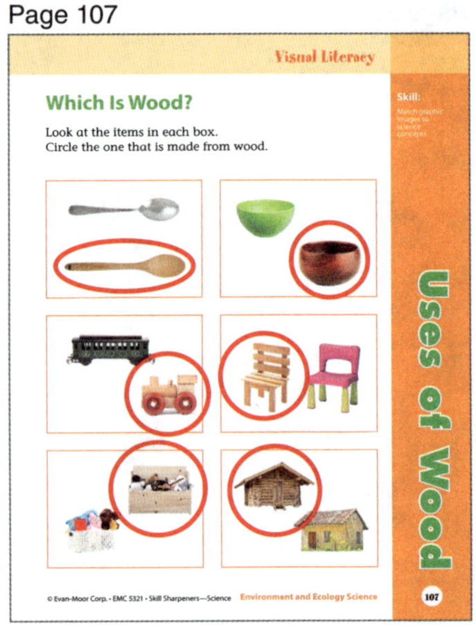
Visual Literacy

Which Is Wood?

Look at the items in each box.
Circle the one that is made from wood.

Skill:

Uses of Wood

© Evan-Moor Corp. • EMC 5321 • Skill Sharpeners—Science · Environment and Ecology Science · 107

Page 108

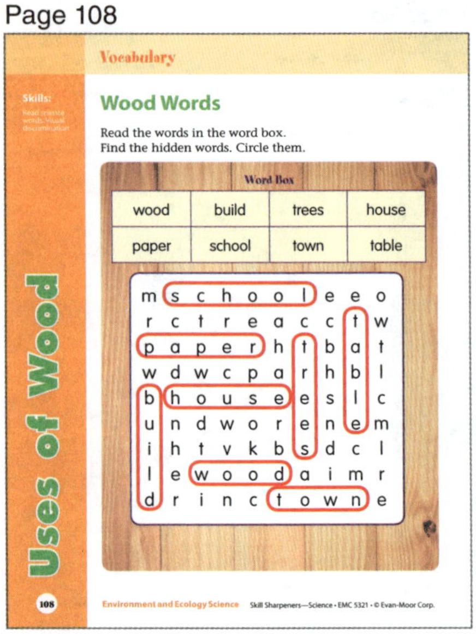
Vocabulary

Wood Words

Read the words in the word box.
Find the hidden words. Circle them.

Word Box

wood	build	trees	house
paper	school	town	table

m s c h o o l e e o
r c t r e a c c t w
p a p e r h t b a t
w d w c p a r h b l
b h o u s e e s l c
u n d w o r e n e m
i h t v k b s d c l
l e w o o d a i m r
d r i n c t o w n e

Skills:

Uses of Wood

108 · Environment and Ecology Science · Skill Sharpeners—Science • EMC 5321 • © Evan-Moor Corp.

Page 109

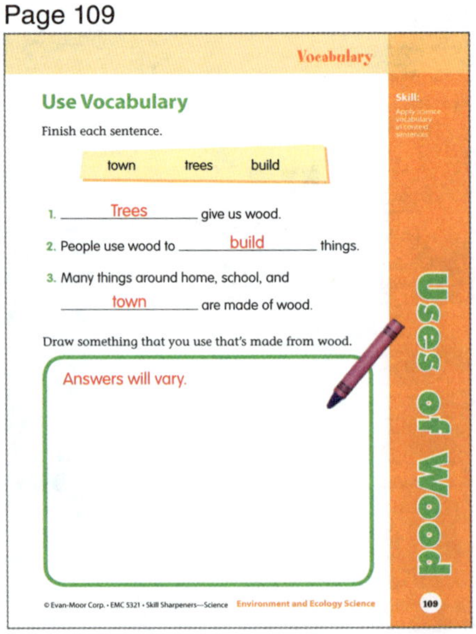
Vocabulary

Use Vocabulary

Finish each sentence.

town trees build

1. Trees give us wood.
2. People use wood to build things.
3. Many things around home, school, and town are made of wood.

Draw something that you use that's made from wood.

Answers will vary.

Skill:

Uses of Wood

© Evan-Moor Corp. • EMC 5321 • Skill Sharpeners—Science · Environment and Ecology Science · 109

Page 110

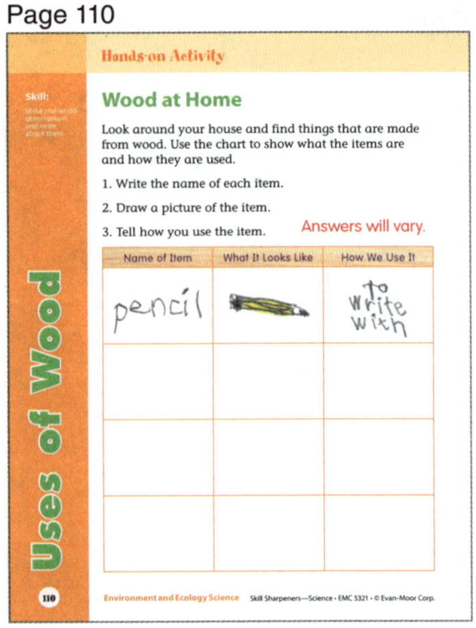
Hands-on Activity

Wood at Home

Look around your house and find things that are made from wood. Use the chart to show what the items are and how they are used.

1. Write the name of each item.
2. Draw a picture of the item.
3. Tell how you use the item.

Answers will vary.

Name of Item	What It Looks Like	How We Use It
pencil		to write with

Skill:

Uses of Wood

110 · Environment and Ecology Science · Skill Sharpeners—Science • EMC 5321 • © Evan-Moor Corp.

Page 114

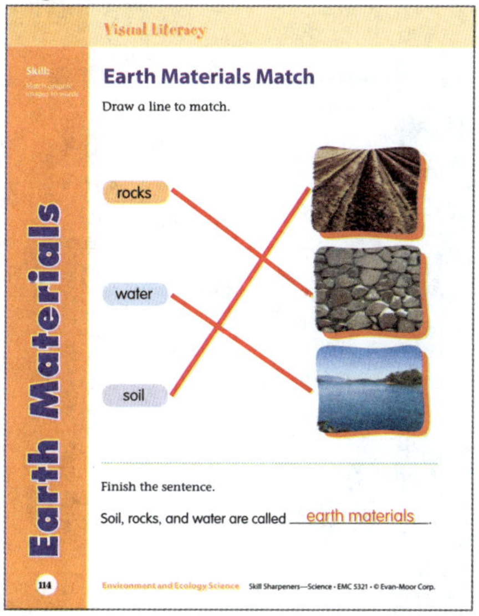
Visual Literacy

Earth Materials

Earth Materials Match

Draw a line to match.

rocks

water

soil

Finish the sentence.

Soil, rocks, and water are called earth materials.

114

Page 115

Visual Literacy

Earth Materials

What Is It?

Make an X on the one that doesn't belong.

rocks

water

soil

115

Page 116

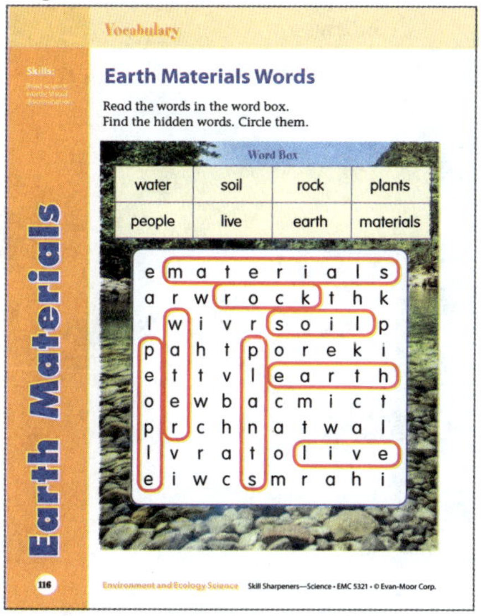
Vocabulary

Earth Materials

Earth Materials Words

Read the words in the word box.
Find the hidden words. Circle them.

Word Box

water	soil	rock	plants
people	live	earth	materials

e m a t e r i a l s
a r w r o c k t h k
l w i v r s o i l p
p a h t p o r e k i
e t t v l e a r t h
o e w b a c m i c t
p r c h n a t w a l
l v r a t o l i v e
e i w c s m r a h i

116

Page 117

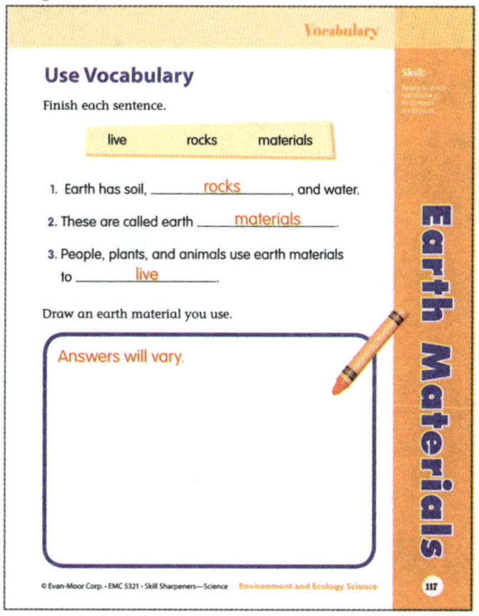
Vocabulary

Earth Materials

Use Vocabulary

Finish each sentence.

live　rocks　materials

1. Earth has soil, rocks, and water.
2. These are called earth materials.
3. People, plants, and animals use earth materials to live.

Draw an earth material you use.

Answers will vary.

117

Page 119

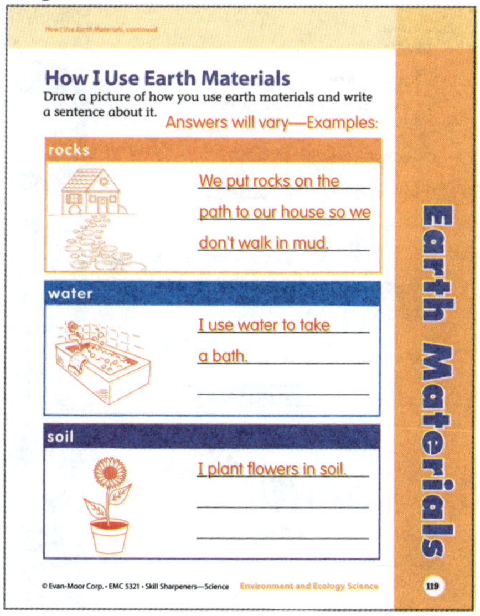
Earth Materials

How I Use Earth Materials

Draw a picture of how you use earth materials and write a sentence about it.

Answers will vary—Examples:

rocks

We put rocks on the path to our house so we don't walk in mud.

water

I use water to take a bath.

soil

I plant flowers in soil.

119

Page 122

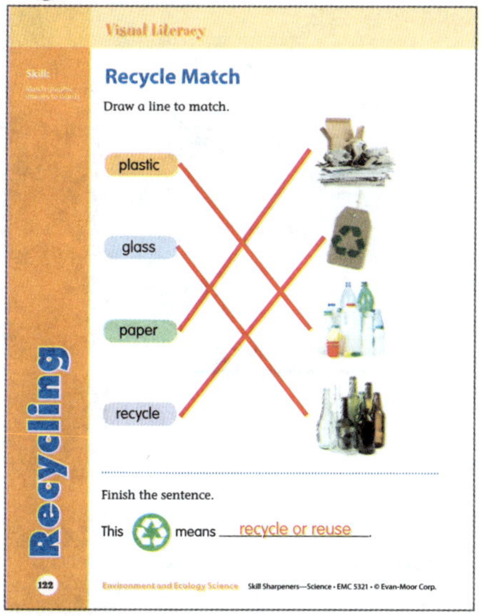
Visual Literacy

Recycling

Recycle Match

Draw a line to match.

plastic

glass

paper

recycle

Finish the sentence.

This ♻ means recycle or reuse.

122

Page 123

Visual Literacy

Recycling

Things to Recycle

Draw a line to match. Put the materials in the correct recycle bin!

Glass　Paper　Plastic

123

Page 124

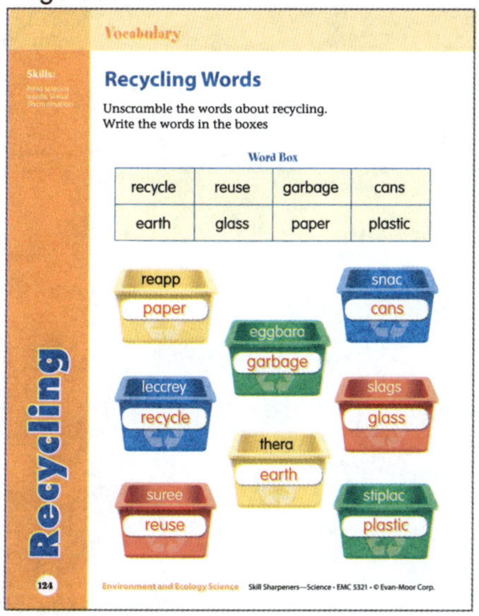
Vocabulary

Recycling

Recycling Words

Unscramble the words about recycling.
Write the words in the boxes.

Word Box

recycle	reuse	garbage	cans
earth	glass	paper	plastic

reapp — paper
snac — cans
eggbara — garbage
leccrey — recycle
slags — glass
thera — earth
suree — reuse
stiplac — plastic

124

Page 125

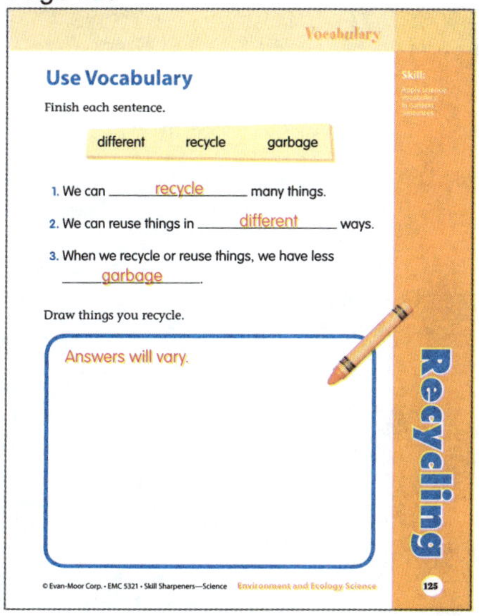
Vocabulary

Recycling

Use Vocabulary

Finish each sentence.

different　recycle　garbage

1. We can recycle many things.
2. We can reuse things in different ways.
3. When we recycle or reuse things, we have less garbage.

Draw things you recycle.

Answers will vary.

125

Page 130

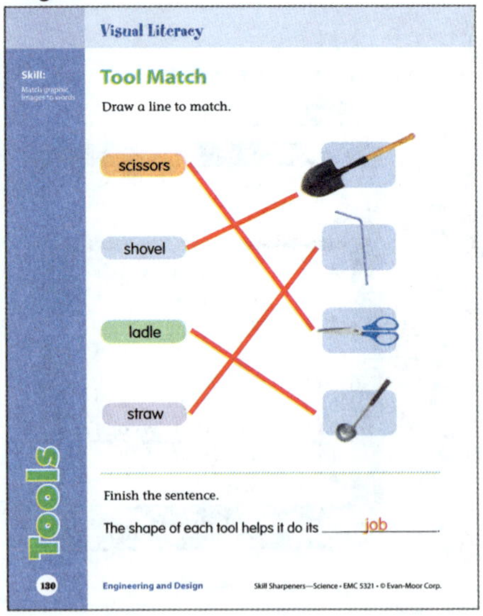

Visual Literacy

Skill:

Tool Match

Draw a line to match.

scissors

shovel

ladle

straw

Finish the sentence.

The shape of each tool helps it do its job

Tools

130 Engineering and Design Skill Sharpeners—Science • EMC 5321 • © Evan-Moor Corp.

Page 131

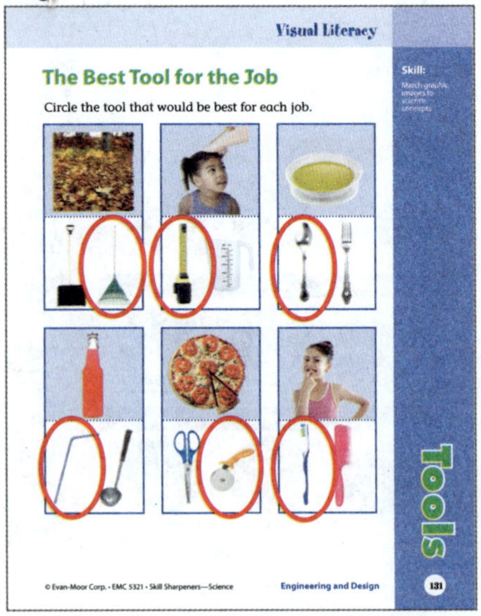

Visual Literacy

The Best Tool for the Job

Circle the tool that would be best for each job.

Skill:

Tools

© Evan-Moor Corp. • EMC 5321 • Skill Sharpeners—Science Engineering and Design 131

Page 132

Vocabulary

Skills:

Tool Words

Read the words in the word box.
Find the hidden words. Circle them.

Word Box

tool	shape	job	different
straw	scissors	shovel	ladle

o	d	i	n	s	h	o	l	r	p
u	i	j	o	b	b	f	f	a	r
h	f	s	t	n	s	h	a	p	e
t	f	s	c	i	s	s	o	r	s
o	e	c	s	o	d	i	b	a	d
o	r	t	t	s	h	o	v	e	l
l	e	c	r	s	y	a	h	f	r
h	n	d	a	l	a	d	l	e	e
a	t	h	w	a	p	e	f	j	o

Tools

132 Engineering and Design Skill Sharpeners—Science • EMC 5321 • © Evan-Moor Corp.

Page 133

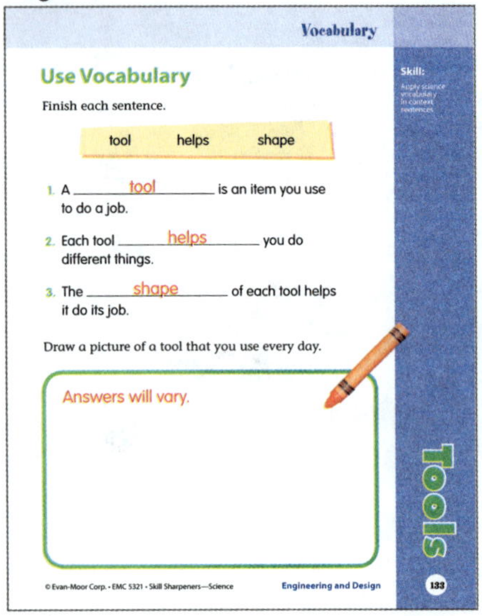

Vocabulary

Use Vocabulary

Finish each sentence.

Skill:

tool helps shape

1. A tool is an item you use to do a job.
2. Each tool helps you do different things.
3. The shape of each tool helps it do its job.

Draw a picture of a tool that you use every day.

Answers will vary.

Tools

© Evan-Moor Corp. • EMC 5321 • Skill Sharpeners—Science Engineering and Design 133

Page 135

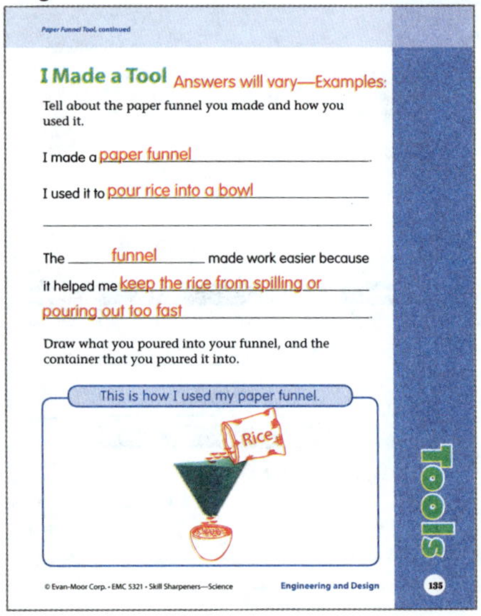

Paper Funnel Tool, continued

I Made a Tool Answers will vary—Examples:

Tell about the paper funnel you made and how you used it.

I made a paper funnel

I used it to pour rice into a bowl

The funnel made work easier because it helped me keep the rice from spilling or pouring out too fast

Draw what you poured into your funnel, and the container that you poured it into.

This is how I used my paper funnel.

Rice

Tools

© Evan-Moor Corp. • EMC 5321 • Skill Sharpeners—Science Engineering and Design 135